Romantic Lovers

The Intimate Marriage

DAVID & CAROLE HOCKING

HARVEST HOUSE PUBLISHERS
Eugene, Oregon 97402

Copyright © 1986 by David and Carole Hocking
Published by Harvest House Publishers
Eugene, Oregon 97402

Library of Congress Catalog Card Number 85-081937
ISBN 0-89081-522-4

Printed in the United States of America.

CONTENTS

The Beauty of Romance

ROMANCE! What a beautiful word! It belongs in every marriage, but so few couples seem to experience it. We feel it at first...uncontrollable sensations, often caused by just a glance or a smile...strong during courtship as we're filled with anticipation in looking forward to that special wedding day!

Why is it that so many couples stop being romantic after the marriage takes place? Why do so few married couples plan dates with each other? Why is it so difficult to be alone, looking into each other's eyes and hearts? Why do the days of our marriages seem so dull, even boring? Why do we take each other for granted? Why do we spend so little time adoring, admiring, and appreciating each other? Why is it easier to compliment someone other than our marital partner?

After years of marital struggle and what we call "quiet tension," we decided to change. It didn't happen overnight; it took time. But it was well worth the effort. We started looking seriously into the Bible for guidance and asking ourselves a lot of questions. We talked with other couples and did some teaching on marriage and family subjects. This effort encouraged us and challenged us. How could we talk to others about "marital bliss" if we were not experiencing it ourselves?

We discovered in our struggles and search that most couples are in desperate need of *romantic love!* We knew about the love of God and that through the Holy Spirit we could know and enjoy that love in our lives. We studied 1 Corinthians 13 diligently, and really tried to apply its principles to what we said and did in our marriage. The more we worked at it, the more it became evident that a certain quality of love was needed between husbands and wives in order to have a marriage the way God intended it to be. It was a very neglected subject as far as we could tell.

Of all the many books on marriage that are available in secular as well as Christian bookstores, none of them can possibly improve on the biblical teaching found in the Song of Solomon. Here is romantic love for married couples that exceeds our greatest dreams and expectations. Here is a manual on sex that beats all secular viewpoints on how a man and a woman should make love. Here is the viewpoint of God Himself, though He is not mentioned by name in the entire book.

Rabbi Aqiba is quoted in the Mishnah with words that declare the excellency and special quality of this romantic song of Solomon:

> In the entire world there is nothing to equal the day
> on which the Song of Solomon was given to Israel.
> All the writings are holy, but the Song of Songs is
> most Holy [1]

Due to his support, all ancient questions about the place of the Song of Solomon in the canon of the Scriptures were silenced.

WHY STUDY THIS BOOK?

That's a good question. As a young boy I was told by older Christians that it was not good to read the book until I was much older. When I got older, I found that many Christians were not sure that the book should be taught or spoken about in public!

Early church leaders, such as Origen and Jerome, refer to a Jewish saying that the Song of Solomon should not be studied by anyone until that person was 30 years of age. Other people are not sure that it should be studied by anyone, regardless of age!

The basic reason for the neglect of this book appears to be the problem of how to interpret it. Is it allegorical or literal? Is it a message about God's love for the believer or is it a historical account of a man and a woman experiencing romantic love? Or is it both?

If you take the book literally (including its symbolic language and poetic descriptions), it appears to be very erotic and sensual. This causes many Christians to avoid the book. At various times in church history, openness about sex was simply prohibited.

G. Lloyd Carr writes in his book *The Song of Solomon*:

> Frankness, openness, tenderness, coupled with ardent longing, explicitly erotic descriptions and intent towards the lover and the beloved, mark the love poetry from all over the ancient Near East. The Song of Solomon is no exception.[2]

The book seems very sensual. Many Christians try to avoid

this fact by applying most of the erotic statements to God's love for believers. To those who know the meaning of the Hebrew words used in this song, it seems incredible that God would express His love for us in such erotic terminology. Surely there is another explanation of this!

S. Craig Glickman wrote in his book *A Song for Lovers*:

Sensuous love with erotic overtones is God's intent for the marriage relationship. The distortion of that relationship has no doubt abased this dimension of life, but that does not justify placing such experience—or Scriptures' Song about it—into the inactive file of living.[3]

The Song of Solomon is sensual—there's no way to escape that conclusion!

INTRIGUING FACTS

To point out that the Song of Solomon is unique is like pointing out that the grass is green or the sky is blue! There are many unusual and interesting facts connected with this book that may help us in interpreting it.

1. There is no direct application or quotation of this book in the entire New Testament.
2. There is no mention of the name of God.
3. There are only 117 verses, with 470 Hebrew words, but 47 of these words appear only in this book and 96 more appear elsewhere less than ten times.
4. There are no theological words or references to religious practices or ceremonies.
5. It is only one song among 1005 which Solomon wrote (cf. 1 Kings 4:32), but it is called "*The* Song

of Songs" in Song of Solomon 1:1. It is the best and the most important of all the songs written by Solomon.

6. The author, Solomon, had 700 wives/princesses, and 300 concubines, women who took his heart away from the Lord (cf. 1 Kings 11:1-4).

CAN WE TRUST WHAT SOLOMON SAYS?

Since Solomon disobeyed God in taking so many wives and concubines, how can we rely upon his teaching and experiences in this Song of Solomon? Is this not the sexual fantasy of a man who did not walk with God? How can he be qualified to write a book on romantic love in marriage?

If Solomon wrote this book after his many marriages, then the book would be a tremendous testimony to the foolishness and tragedy of such a lifestyle. This romantic poem emphasizes what marital love should really be like, and that God's standard is one man and one woman totally in love with each other.

Even if Solomon were already involved in polygamous relationships (which were in fact political alliances with the nations surrounding him), this would not necessarily disqualify him from describing how a person should really conduct himself in marriage. It might even intensify the importance of what he teaches in this book.

The truth is that we have no way of knowing how old Solomon was at the time or whether his lifestyle had already degenerated into the tragedies of his later years. The remark in Song of Solomon 6:8 about "sixty queens and eighty concubines, and virgins without number" does not indicate that this is the number of women he had at the time. In fact, the text does not say "*I have* 60 queens, etc." but "*there are* 60 queens, etc." It is a poetic device for comparing his bride with all the other women of the world. He is declaring her to be the best among them all.

WHICH INTERPRETATION?

Glickman quotes a volume written on the history of the Song of Solomon during the Middle Ages:

> Over five hundred commentaries on the song remain with us from the first seventeen hundred years alone. Yet after these five hundred and perhaps more, the Westminster Assembly observed in 1657 that the commentaries customarily increased the cloud of obscurity they had hoped to remove.[4]

There are two basic ways to interpret the Song of Solomon: symbolically and historically (literally). The symbolic approach usually takes one of two possible viewpoints:

1. The book pictures Jehovah's love for Israel.
2. The book pictures Jesus Christ's love for the church.

Because of the teaching of Ephesians 5:22-33, many Christians take the second viewpoint. Jesus Christ is the Bridegroom, and the church is the bride. However, since there are no references to the Song of Solomon in the New Testament, many interpreters believe that it simply pictures God's love for His people Israel (also called a "bride"). Many Jewish commentators also take this view.

The second way to interpret the book makes more sense in terms of the actual statements of the book and the meaning of the words used in the text. The historical or literal view believes that the bridegroom is Solomon or some unnamed shepherd lover who seems to get in the way of Solomon's plans to have this woman. The majority of commentators believe that the lover is Solomon, presenting himself in the prime of life and describing his first love and his only divinely authorized wife.

There is some disagreement over the bride in this love song, summarized by three major viewpoints about this woman:

1. She is one of his wives
   (not important to know her identity).
2. She is the daughter of Pharaoh
   (cf. 1 Kings 3:1; 7:8; 9:16; Song of Solomon 1:9).
3. She is Abishag
   (1 Kings 1:1-4; 2:13-25).

The daughter-of-Pharaoh viewpoint makes her a Gentile woman and is usually supported by those who wish to see in this song a connection with the church of Jesus Christ, the Gentile bride. Solomon seems to have a special attraction for this woman and even built her a house. But the need for an alliance with Egypt was critical. It is doubtful that this woman is the woman of the Song of Solomon, in spite of the reference to a prize mare among Pharaoh's chariots in Song of Solomon 1:9. According to 1 Kings 9:16, Pharaoh was involved in military actions in the land of Israel, and it is more likely to believe that his daughter whom Solomon married was simply a political link that guaranteed the peace and good relationships of the two countries.

A WORD ABOUT ABISHAG

First Kings 1:1-4 introduces us to a beautiful woman who spent her youth in the fields, working vineyards. In a nationwide search for a lovely young woman to lie beside the elderly king David and serve his needs during his dying years, Abishag was chosen. She came from an area called Shunam, presumably located in Galilee. There is a site near Mount Tabor in Galilee's Esdraelon Valley called Shunem. It is about nine miles west of Megiddo. Attempts to pinpoint this historical fact have proven fruitless. The truth is that we simply do not know where this young woman was raised.

The Bible is clear (1 Kings 1:4) in telling us that her virginity was not taken away by the elderly king David. Her ministry to him in his closing days was completely a matter of physical care, not sexual pleasure.

Solomon, of course, was also a part of that home. He had plenty of opportunity to observe this beautiful young woman as she cared for his dying father. He became deeply attached to her, and when his brother Adonijah tried to get his mother's approval for taking Abishag as a wife (since he lost the kingdom to Solomon), Solomon was enraged. He gave the order to Benaiah his executioner to kill Adonijah for this request, and it was done. Obviously Solomon had a great love for Abishag. He refused to give her up to his brother Adonijah. In having his brother killed over this, it becomes obvious that the real love of Solomon's heart is Abishag, the Shunammite.

Abishag was not a lady of the royal courts. She was a country girl, and the Song of Solomon makes continual reference to this fact. She worked in the fields under the hot sun, and was not used to the beautiful clothes, expensive jewelry, and exotic perfumes of the nobility. But she was what we might call a "natural beauty." And Solomon loved her with all his heart. He wrote his most important song about his love for her, and under the inspiration of the Holy Spirit has left for all of us a standard to follow in expressing love to our spouses.

SYMBOLIC AND HISTORICAL?

It is very possible that, while the primary meaning of the Song of Solomon is the romantic love of husband and wife, a secondary meaning might be seen in God's love for us. We must be careful not to press every detail and erotic imagery of this romantic love song to imply a characteristic of God's love for us; and yet Luke 24:44 reveals that all of Scripture speaks in some way of the glory and beauty of our Messiah Himself, the Lord Jesus Christ:

These are the words which I spoke to you while I was still with you, that all things must be fulfilled which were written in the Law of Moses and the Prophets and the Psalms concerning Me.

The Hebrew Old Testament is divided into three parts: the Law, the Prophets, and the Writings, of which Psalms is the first in the list of books called "the Writings." The Song of Solomon is one of "the Writings." Therefore in some sense the book speaks of Jesus Christ, since our Lord said that all of the books are "concerning Me."

It is proper to seek the beauty of the great Bridegroom in the Song of Solomon. Solomon is a historical type of Jesus Christ in that sense.

While we will refer at times to this symbolical interpretation, our primary focus will be on the literal interpretation of the book as a romantic love song, describing the historical relationship of Solomon and Abishag and thus demonstrating to all future generations the standards by which every marriage should be governed and blessed by God.

Carole and I believe that this book should be studied by every couple seeking to be married. It should be the manual we recommend in premarital counselling. It should also be the manual which married couples use throughout their married life and rely on for advice regarding romantic love. Every couple struggling with their marriage should flee to this book for renewal and restoration. It contains the kind of relationship which will make every marriage grow. It will teach every couple how to have a fully satisfying marital experience, where love dominates and romance flourishes.

Questions about sex are answered in this book. The secular world has bombarded us with its opinions, and has encouraged us toward easy divorce and illicit affairs. It has tried to sell us on the glories of promiscuity and has spoken frequently on the joys of adulterous relationships. It has attempted to justify and defend the individual's right to explore sexual fantasy and passion without moral restraint or divine authority. It is critical of Christian viewpoints and biblical teachings on sex and marriage, but it has done nothing to improve our marriages or satisfy the longings of our hearts. The exploitation of sex in our culture is a major factor in the breakup of marriages and families. We have sown the wind, and we now reap the whirlwind.

It's time for a change! We need to return to the Bible, and in particular the Song of Solomon. There we will find help for our struggling marriages and our unfulfilled desires. In its words we will find encouragement to love again. We will feel motivated to be romantic the way God intended. We may blush with the frankness of biblical sensuality, but we will be challenged to rethink our own opinions about marital sex.

If you want another chance at your dying marriage...this book is for you!

If you want help for a dull, boring, and empty marriage...this book is for you!

If you want to increase your love for your spouse...this book is for you!

If you want to strengthen your sexual understanding...this book is for you!

If you want to be romantic again...this book is for you!

If you want to know what God approves of
in a marriage...this book is for you!

If you want to get married soon...
this book is for you!

If you want to see how much God loves you...
this book is for you!

Our sincere prayer is that our viewpoints expressed in this study of the Song of Solomon will bring understanding, healing, love, growth, and encouragement to all who read it and apply its marvelous principles. We have found this book to be a tremendous blessing in our own marriage. We hope you experience this too!

[1] G. Lloyd Carr, *The Song of Solomon*, p. 17.
[2] Ibid., p. 39.
[3] S. Craig Glickman, *A Song for Lovers*, p. 9.
[4] Ibid., p. 173.

1 How to Know if You Have Fallen in Love

SONG OF SOLOMON • 1:1-4

Couples who fall in love with each other speak of the intensity of their emotional responses toward each other. They long for each other's presence and affection. When they are apart, they experience pain, loneliness, and emptiness.

The young lady standing in front of me after one of my sermons seemed deeply concerned. She was lovely, talented, and intensely interested in spiritual matters. Her problem? She wanted to know how a person falls in love. Specifically, she wanted information on whether her feelings for a certain man were the kind that led toward marriage.

I told her that in a few weeks I would be speaking on that subject. She said, "I can't wait that long." When I inquired as to why, she said, "He just asked me to marry him." So much for patience!

People seem to be falling out of love as surely as falling in love these days. One man of 35 told me that he did not love his wife anymore: "I have fallen out of love with her." I replied, "That's not a big problem." He seemed surprised at my answer. "Why do you say that?" I continued, "Because you can learn to love her again. Just as you have fallen out of love with her, so you can fall in love with her again." But he didn't want to hear this because, as time proved, he had already "fallen in love" with another woman. I get tired of this story—it seems like a broken record that keeps repeating the same line!

THE SYMPTOMS OF FALLING IN LOVE

There are many married couples who have never "fallen in love" with each other. They need to, but in so many cases they remain apathetic to the necessity of such romance. Their marriage is based on duty and responsibility, which of course is essential. But if all a couple has going for them is the fact of a past ceremony, a couple of kids, and a few years under their belt, they are living together in a relationship that is less than what God intended. Romantic love is needed in every marriage. The Song of Solomon makes that fact abundantly clear!

Marriage is based on commitment, not romance. If no romance ever exists in a marriage, it is still a marriage in the sight of God if the man and the woman have spoken vows to each other before two or three witnesses. Marriages should be held together even if no romance exists. But as we read the Song of Solomon we become increasingly aware of the fact that God intended marriages to be filled with romantic love.

Couples who fall in love with each other speak of the intensity of their emotional responses toward each other. They long for each other's presence and affection. When they are apart, they experience pain, loneliness, and emptiness.

When you fall in love you are often blind to the other person's faults and weaknesses. You may know what some of them are, but it makes no difference to you. You never refer to them and find yourself quite protective of them in the presence of other people.

Falling in love means that you get excited at the very mention of your lover's name. There's no one on earth with whom you would rather share your time, money, and life. You look forward to the next time you can look into that person's eyes and feel again what you felt the first time it happened to you. You are in love, and it feels so wonderful!

FALLING IN LOVE WITH WHOM?

What if you fall in love with someone other than your mate? This is a very important issue, especially for Christians who claim to be under the authority of the Bible and God Himself. It happens—people do fall in love with individuals other than their spouses.

When it happened to John, he interpreted it wrongly from the start; he thought it meant that this was the will of God: "God wouldn't have let this happen if it were not His will. Besides, I wasn't looking for someone else. . .it just happened."

Our feelings are quite mysterious at times. Why do we respond to certain people with romantic love when we were not intending to do so? Is God behind this? If it means leaving your husband or your wife, the answer is *absolutely not!* God never causes us to fall in love with another person in order to get us out of a bad marriage or to give us "someone we really deserve."

We can frustrate ourselves greatly by trying to analyze the "why" behind our feelings. The fact is that we can fall in love with people other than our mates quite easily. The real question is "What should we do when this happens?"

For one thing, we should immediately renew our minds

with the teaching of God's Word about marital fidelity and commitment to our families no matter what—for better or for worse. Secondly, we should recognize the danger of our feelings and the possibility that we could fall into sin if we continue to foster that relationship and encourage the fulfillment of our desires for that person. No matter how strong our feelings might be, the Bible is clear on what we should avoid—sexual immorality.

It is also crucial to recognize that romantic feeling by itself is never an adequate guideline for human behavior. We can be deceived easily by its presence and its effects upon our emotional makeup. A marriage must be based on much more than this, for a relationship that depends upon romantic love alone will eventually wither and die.

HELP FROM SOLOMON?

The best help on the need for romantic love within a marriage is found in the Song of Solomon. This is romance par excellence! It is also good advice for the unmarried. Singles desperately need help on this matter because of the intense pressure that a single lifestyle places upon an individual.

Everybody seems to be searching for romantic love these days. People want to fall in love and to experience romance that is often found only in novels or movies. They picture in their minds the ideal situation in which boy meets girl and both go bananas over each other!

But Solomon gives God's viewpoint, and that's vitally important! The secular world speaks much of romantic love but offers very few guidelines for true love. Morals and ethics are usually left out. Solomon tells you how "falling in love" should happen when God's love is controlling and when His principles determine your feelings.

THE SONG OF SONGS

The Song of songs, which is Solomon's.

What an opening line to the most powerful romantic story ever written! It tells us several things. It speaks of music; it is a song—not just an ordinary song, but *The* Song of Songs! Romantic love done in God's way is filled with music—the music of love!

Musical songs are poetic, and the Song of Solomon is saturated with romantic poetry and beautiful vocabulary. It tells us how couples who are in love communicate with each other. There is nothing here of crass, blunt, sarcastic, or critical talk. It is sweet and refreshing to the heart.

This is one song with 117 verses. It should be read as a whole and captured in our heart as though every line were essential to its impact and importance. There are not many songs in this book, but only one—The Song of Songs.

Mary and Henry had been married for six years, but now things were going sour. Critical words passed between them on a daily basis, and neither one of them was happy with the results. Both wanted to change but didn't know where to begin. It's hard to admit we're wrong and start over!

When I asked them about their communication with each other, I knew I was on the right track. They both admitted that it was not good. Some of their difficulty began with the kind of communication they shared while making love. They had not been Christians for very long, and the words they used with each other came from the streets, not from the heart of God. I shared some of the verses from Solomon's Song with them, and they both started laughing. I admit that it does seem a little strange at first. After some explanation and a few more passages, they started to settle down and pay attention to the romance of this book.

This story has a happy ending. Mary and Henry decided

to read the Song of Solomon repeatedly and to begin to communicate with each other along the lines of this beautiful love song. In a few weeks their relationship was radically changed, and today they are very happy.

Sexual communication today has become ugly. Sexual aggressiveness and violent intentions have been promoted by our culture, and obscenity is often expressed by couples in the secrecy of the bedroom. How tragic!

But it doesn't have to be that way. It is so much more rewarding and healthy for a couple to speak romantically as Solomon and Abishag did in this beautiful love song. The words we use today may be more contemporary than those used 3000 years ago, but they should be the very best and beautiful of all that we know and have.

WHAT DO YOU CALL YOUR SPOUSE?

Do you call your spouse "honey," "sugar," "darling," "sweetheart," "precious," etc.? We all have our special names and nicknames. They often reveal the kind of relationship we have with each other. Even the inflection of the voice tells us a great deal. The sound level often says whether our attitude is sweet or negative.

Solomon calls Abishag "my love" (Hebrew *raah*) in several passages (1:9,15; 2:2,10,13; 4:1,7; 5:2; 6:4). The word is translated in many different ways in the English Bible, but the primary emphasis would be on *friendship*. The root meaning of the word is "to guard, care for, tend." His friendship is controlled by deep concern for her protection and well-being. The New International Version of the Bible uses the words "my darling."

When a man truly loves a woman, he expresses his desire to be a loving friend who will care for her and her needs. He cannot remain apathetic to her concerns. He desires to see things from her point of view. That takes patience and time.

He longs to take her heart into his hands and caress it gently and tenderly. He wants her to know that whatever she feels he wants to feel, and that he wants to do all he can to help her. That's romantic love!

Abishag calls Solomon "my beloved" 27 times in this book (Hebrew *dodi*). The daughters of Jerusalem use the term on five occasions. Another form of the word (*dodim*) appears four times and refers to lovemaking, and is usually translated with the simple word "love." An example is in 1:2: "Your love is better than wine." She is referring to his lovemaking or his sexual love (cf. 1:4; 4:10; 7:12).

All of this is quite amazing in the light of common criticism which women give toward men. Most women are not very thrilled with the lovemaking skills of men. Husbands are often abrupt, quick, and selfish. Women desire tenderness, patience, and romance. They want to be swept off their feet, but their husbands can't find the broom!

WHERE ARE THE LOVERS?

The Song of Solomon portrays the man as the lover. He is the romantic one: tender in his approach, lavish in his praise, sensitive to his spouse's needs. Abishag refers to Solomon as her lover; it is her favorite word. She, like women today, has a need for the romance of her husband, and she expresses throughout the book how much it means to her.

Solomon is an example to all husbands today. We need to be romantic toward our wives. Constant encouragement and praise must flow from our lips as we relate to our wives and describe their attractiveness to our hearts. It is not a mere feminine quality to be romantic. "Macho" men can learn to be romantic! It is not so much the bringing of the flowers or candy or expensive gifts that makes us romantic, but our *communication*. Specifically, it is the way we respond to each other and describe the assets and attractiveness of each other.

HOW TO KNOW IF YOU HAVE FALLEN IN LOVE

*Let him kiss me with the kisses of his mouth—
for your love is better than wine. Because
of the fragrance of your good ointments,
your name is ointment poured forth;
therefore the virgins love you. Lead me away!
We will run after you. The king has brought
me into his chambers. We will be glad
and rejoice in you. We will remember
your love more than wine.*

These verses present three ways in which we can know if we have fallen in love. They speak from the wife's point of view.

1. When his caresses (lovemaking) are more desirable than any celebration (1:2).
2. When his character is more desirable than his cologne.
3. When his companionship is more desirable than the company of all other people (1:4).

ABOUT THOSE CARESSES

Carole and I met when she was in her final year of college and I was in my first year of seminary. We were in the same car with two other people traveling home to California from Indiana to spend the Christmas holidays. On the return trip (we were driving straight through) at about 3:00 A.M., I happened to look in the rearview mirror to the backseat. Carole was wide awake, and our eyes met through that mirror. I'll never forget the feeling: We fell in love! Though no words were exchanged between us, and it was days before we met again (and weeks before I was ever able to hold her hand), we both felt it that night—romantic love. What a feeling it was and is!

Several weeks later I had the joy of holding her in my arms and kissing her. I asked her to marry me that same night. What a thrill! Just touching her was sheer ecstasy to me!

> *Let him kiss me with the kisses of his mouth—for your love is better than wine.*

Two things are clear from this verse:

1. *Sexual love is initiated by the man.*

She says "Let him kiss me" and refers to his "love" (lovemaking). In a marriage designed by God, the husband is the one who initiates sexual love. This does not mean that the wife should avoid all opportunities to initiate sexual love with her husband, but it does emphasize the importance of the husband's leadership.

As a representative of the love of Jesus Christ (cf. Ephesians 5:25-33), the husband should be the initiator. It is Jesus Christ who initiates love toward us, even when we do not respond to Him (Romans 5:8). Our capacity to love is based on His love for us (1 John 4:19). Many husbands need to understand this important fact about sexual love.

2. *Sexual love is to be enjoyed.*

Abishag spoke of his lovemaking as being better than wine, the symbol of enjoyment and celebration. This wife sees her husband's sexual responses to her as better than any human celebration on earth!

Many Christian couples are not sure of what the Bible says about sexual pleasure. We are all aware of how much enjoyment we can receive while engaged in it, but some of us are not sure if it is carnal or spiritual. Hebrews 13:4 should clarify this point for all of us:

> *Marriage is honorable among all and the bed undefiled.*

The word "bed" (Greek *coitus*) refers to sexual intercourse. The last part of the verse speaks about God's judgment upon fornicators and adulterers. The clear implication is that sexual pleasures between husband and wife are legitimate and honorable practices before God. As a matter of fact, God invented sex, not *Playboy* magazine!

Ann saw one of our women counselors about the problems that she and Jack were having. She briefly told me that she was not being fulfilled by Jack's lovemaking skills, and wondered if we had anyone who could help her. One of our ladies listened to her story, and then told me I ought to see Jack. It seems that he reacted adversely to sex for pleasure, believing that it was only a necessary duty in order to propagate the human race!

The day we talked is still fresh in my mind. It was unusual in one sense: Most men do not have this problem. Jack had been raised in a very strict and religious home. He had been taught this view of sex since he was a child, and he firmly believed it. When I inquired about whether he had any desire to give or receive pleasure through sexual involvement with his wife, he said that he did but that he always tried to confess it immediately to God and suppress it in his mind and heart.

Frankly, I was delighted to deal with a person like Jack. He really loved the Lord and was greatly loved by his wife, Ann. They needed a biblical answer. When I showed him Hebrews 13:4, he was amazed. When we read a few of the passages in the Song of Solomon, he seemed embarrassed. I asked him what he thought. I've always appreciated his answer: "It's none of your business, but I think I would like to talk to my wife about it." We both agreed, and had prayer together.

A few weeks later I spotted them in church, and by the smile on his wife's face I knew that things had improved. After the service he said to me, "Pastor, I'm finding it hard these days to leave the house for work!"

Are you still excited about the caresses of your spouse? People in love can't wait to touch each other again. Carole and I have a little ritual at mealtime: We always pray for our food before we eat, and hold hands while praying; then immediately after the "amen," we kiss each other. An older couple taught us to do this many years ago, and we are still at it. We love to touch each other every day. We need each other's affection. When our romance dwindles, so does our affection.

HOW DOES HE SMELL?

The second evidence that you are in love is when his character is more desirable than his cologne!

Because of the fragrance of your good ointments, your name is ointment poured forth.

The word "name" refers to his character, not merely his title. "David" in Hebrew means "beloved" or "lover." I hope that my character reveals the meaning of my name. "Carole" means "joyful song," and her temperament and inward spirit seem to reflect the meaning of her name.

We both use perfumes, but the perfumes we use are not worthy to be compared with the smell of the heart. What we are really like in our hearts is much more important than our outward appearance or smell. Couples in love are attracted by the personality of the spouse. Ecclesiastes 7:1 says, "A good name [character] is better than precious ointment." How true!

ALONE AT LAST!

When you are in love, you treasure the moments alone. You can't wait to be together, away from all other people. The third characteristic of lovers focuses on intimate companionship. When his companionship is more desirable than the company of all others, you are in love!

Song of Solomon 1:4 is difficult to interpret. It is hard to know who is speaking as well as what is being said. The "daughters of Jerusalem" mentioned in 1:5 are speaking in this verse. Abishag refers to the "virgins" who love Solomon (1:3). In the New King James Version the verse says:

> *Lead* me *away!* We *will run after you.*
> *The king has brought* me *into his chambers.*
> We *will be glad and rejoice in you.*
> We *will remember your love more than wine.*

The first statement is said by Abishag. The next implies that a group is speaking ("we"). However, the Hebrew can be translated "Let us run together," meaning that Abishag is asking Solomon to come with her. That translation is preferred. She reveals her desire to be alone with him, to spend time together. She then mentions that he responds by inviting her to his chambers in order to be alone with her. Couples in love want to be alone with each other.

The daughters of Jerusalem (ladies of the court) speak in the latter half of the verse and express their excitement and joy over the qualities of Solomon, and especially his love. They refer to her opening words about his love being better than wine: "We will remember your love more than wine."

Abishag treasures her privacy with Solomon, knowing full well how others think of him and enjoy his company as well. When you are in love you become quite possessive (rightly so) and cannot wait until you can be alone again with the one you love.

Couples who have no time to be alone with each other are making a big mistake. It affects the quality of their marriage whether they want to admit it or not. Every couple needs to plan time together alone. After the children are born, the pressures and struggles for privacy are increased.

But the need remains, and sometimes even gets stronger. If not fulfilled by your spouse, someone else often fills the need, and more serious difficulties arise that often lead to divorce.

ARE YOU IN LOVE?

Take the following test:

1. I want to be touched, caressed, and loved by my spouse more than any other human activity or event.

YES_____ NO_____

2. I find my spouse's inward spirit, attitudes, and character more attractive than his or her outward appearance, including clothes, cosmetics, and physical body.

YES_____ NO_____

3. I would rather be alone with my spouse than enjoy the company of anyone else on earth.

YES_____ NO_____

If you don't score too well (less than three "yes" answers), don't give up—there's hope for you in the message of the Song of Solomon!

2 | What Makes a Woman Beautiful?

SONG OF SOLOMON • 1:5-11

A husband's words of praise and encouragement are what makes a wife beautiful. She sees herself through his eyes. When he thinks she is special, she starts believing it herself.

---

beautiful poem is found in Proverbs 31:10-31 describing the traits of a virtuous wife. It contains 22 verses, one for each letter of the Hebrew alphabet. Each verse begins with a word whose first letter is the next consecutive letter of the Hebrew alphabet.

If we would put that style of poetry into English, it would go something like this:

Verse 1: *All* that she reflects is beauty and love.
Verse 2: *Beauty* is her constant portion.
Verse 3: *Captivating* are all her ways.
Verse 4: *D...*

Poetry varies in style, but a common reason behind it is

to express one's emotions, and often to be romantic.

Carole has received poems from her lover and husband from time to time, such as—

Roses are red, violets are blue;
There's no one on earth as sweet as you!

Not a whole lot of creativity, but you get the idea!

Solomon is going to use many beautiful words and illustrations to tell the love of his heart, Abishag, how beautiful she is to him. In one sense, a husband's words of praise and encouragement are what makes a wife beautiful. She sees herself through his eyes. When he thinks she is special, she starts believing it herself. When he is critical and judgmental of her attitudes, actions, or appearance, her self-esteem drops and she loses a sense of her beauty that he must provide.

DARK BUT LOVELY!

In verses 5-7 of chapter 1, Abishag gives her evaluations of herself. She is insecure and obviously not comfortable around the courtyards of Solomon's palace in Jerusalem. She comes from the fields, not the polished stones of city life. Listen carefully to her heart as she talks about herself:

I am dark, but lovely, O daughters of Jerusalem, like the tents of Kedar, like the curtains of Solomon. Do not look upon me, because I am dark, because the sun has tanned me. My mother's sons were angry with me; they made me the keeper of the vineyards, but my own vineyard I have not kept. Tell me, O you whom I love, where you feed your flock, where you make it rest at noon. For why should I be as one who veils herself by the flocks of your companions?

She recognized the facts about her appearance and accepted them.

She had a sense of self-esteem and self-acceptance. Though feeling somewhat insecure, she knew exactly who she was, and she wanted her lover to understand that fact.

Couples who are dating are frequently manipulative in their actions as they try to put their best foot forward. The man wants the woman to know his strengths, not his weaknesses, and the woman wants the man to know how great she is, not how she struggles with many things in life. As is frequently said, "Love is blind." That's so true when we fall in love with another person!

Jim was a good man, but he had some difficulties in social grace and charm, so he was so glad to finally have a girlfriend. For many years he had wanted one, but in God's timing his first love came in his early thirties. He was really afraid that this girl would find out about his clumsiness and awkwardness in public, and eventually drop him. So we talked about this one day. I encouraged him to be open and honest in his relationship with her—not to deceive her in any way, but rather to allow the Lord to build their relationship on truth and complete acceptance.

One night while they were out to dinner, he shared his problems with her and acknowledged that he would understand if she did not want to continue the relationship. Much to his surprise, she already knew about his weaknesses, and because he openly shared them with her she loved him all the more. They eventually got married.

Self-acceptance is important. We must learn to recognize who we are before God, and also that we are special to Him and unique among all people. We don't have to impress the one we love by deceitful actions and words. We don't have to cover up who we are. It is far better that couples know each other's personalities and peculiarities before the wedding than after.

Two things are apparent in the self-acceptance of this lovely lady:

1. *She insisted that she was beautiful even if she did not look exactly like everyone else.*

She addresses the daughters of Jerusalem in this evaluation of herself. We believe that these ladies are those raised in the courts, not the fields. They were accustomed to elaborate surroundings, expensive clothing and jewelry, exotic perfumes, and soft skin that was unexposed to the rays of the sun. They were sheltered and protected. Abishag's life had been much different.

The "daughters of Jerusalem" are used in this romantic love song as a kind of choral response. In addition to verse 5 of chapter 1, they appear in 2:7, 3:5,10; 5:8,16; and 8:4.

Some commentators see these women as a part of the king's harem, and speak of jealousy and envy in their relationship with Abishag. Song of Solomon 6:8 has often been used to try to prove this point. It speaks of 60 queens, 80 concubines, and virgins without number. Some believe that this is Solomon's harem at the writing of the Song of Solomon. But the text does not indicate that these belong to Solomon. It is a poetic device (increasing number combined with decreasing position in life) indicating that Abishag is the only woman of his heart among so many who might be available from all over the world.

Some interpreters believe that the daughters of Jerusalem are the bridal attendants and also the "virgins" of 1:3, and of course this is possible.

Whoever these women are, they were different in attitude and appearance from Abishag, Solomon's love. Abishag knew this quite well, but still insisted that in spite of her differences and difficult circumstances, she was lovely.

2. *She illustrated her beauty in persuasive ways.*

In 1:5 she compares her own beauty to the "tents of Kedar" and the "curtains of Solomon." The "tents of Kedar" were covered with black goat's hair, like the Bedouins still use today.

Though black, as her skin was, there was a beauty about them on a hillside that speaks of mystery and enchantment. The "curtains of Solomon" were designed by the finest artisans in the world, and the fabrics and colors were indeed beautiful. The "tents" were outside, under the stars; the "curtains" were inside the palace. Perhaps she is describing herself in the same way: what she is like on the outside as well as on the inside. In any case, she makes her point: "dark, but lovely."

She responded to the opinions of other people with honesty and integrity.

The qualities of her life are beginning to take shape in these early words of the Song of Songs. She is characterized by self-acceptance, and now also by honesty. She states clearly the reasons why her skin is so dark in comparison to the other ladies of the court. She is up-front about herself, and that is a quality to be admired. Her reasons for being dark are threefold:

1. *Exposure to the sun:* "Because the sun has tanned me."
2. *Attitudes of her family:* "My mother's sons were angry with me; they made me the keeper of the vineyards."
3. *Lack of opportunities:* "My own vineyard I have not kept."

References to her mother are found in 3:4; 6:9; and 8:1,2. Since her father is never mentioned, we assume that he died. This would explain why her brothers are telling her what to do. We will also learn from chapter 8 that they were watching out for her well-being while she was growing up.

They kept her in the fields, and the sun darkened her skin during those early years of her life. It could not shield her beauty, however. When a search was made throughout the land of Israel for the most beautiful woman possible to comfort King David in his dying days, the search committee did not overlook Abishag even though the sun had darkened her skin thoroughly.

The reference she made to her "own vineyard" is no doubt a statement about her appearance. She did not have time to pay much attention to items like cosmetics and clothing. She was a "natural beauty," simple, yet gorgeous—rugged, yet lovely.

She resisted all appearances of evil and immorality.

In addition to self-acceptance and honesty, one of the most admirable traits of this young lady was that of integrity in terms of moral purity. She was quite concerned about appearances and suggestions of wrongdoing. Her words in 1:7 are addressed to Solomon: "Tell me, O you whom I love." It was her love for him that caused her to be careful about public contacts.

She was most insistent that he tell her where she should meet him. She had no desire to veil herself as prostitutes did. She did not want to wander through the streets and fields looking for him. This would not only be embarrassing but demeaning. She wanted everything to be right. She was in love, and its strength was deeper than those today who allow passion to dictate and lust to control.

I HAVE COMPARED YOU, MY LOVE!

After hearing his sweetheart open her heart and speak honestly about her past circumstances and present feelings, Solomon is quick to bring his encouragement, a quality about him which will continue to grow in this romantic love song. Song of Solomon 1:8-11 gives us his first words:

If you do not know, O fairest among women, follow in the footsteps of the flock, and feed your little goats beside the shepherd's tents. I have compared you, my love, to my filly among Pharaoh's chariots. Your

*cheeks are lovely with ornaments, your neck
with chains of gold. We will make you ornaments
of gold with studs of silver.*

One of the problems connected with the interpretation of
the Song of Solomon is being able to identify clearly who is
speaking. In two places (5:9 and 6:1), the daughters of Jerusalem use the phrase "O fairest among women." Does this mean
that they are the ones speaking in 1:8?

It would seem that this verse comes from the lips of Solomon himself. He is encouraging her in how they could meet
together or in the fact that he would take care of her problem (mentioned in 1:7). She need not worry about it. He would
handle the other "shepherds" or "companions."

The phrase "O fairest among women" spoken by the
daughters of Jerusalem in 5:9 and 6:1 can be seen as a reference to what Solomon says in this opening chapter.

Solomon does three things in order to encourage his beautiful lover. All husbands need to encourage their wives, and
perhaps even make a list of what to say and do in order to
accomplish that goal. Here's a simple one I made for Carole
one day when I felt she was a little down.

1. Pray for her at the beginning of each hour today.
2. Call her at midmorning for no reason but to say "I love
   you."
3. Surprise her by taking her to lunch (call one hour
   ahead).
4. Take her shopping and buy her a dress.
5. Tell her tonight in bed how she has blessed my life.

You can come up with your own list! Consider carefully
what Solomon did for Abishag.

He relieved her concerns.

He did this in two ways. He first of all described the place
she had in his heart:

O fairest among women.

The word "fairest" means "beautiful." Solomon let her know that she was the best among beauties.

Secondly, he clearly directed her as to what she should do and where she could go so that they could be together without embarrassment or suspicion:

> *Follow in the footsteps of the flock, and feed your little goats beside the shepherds' tents.*

No one would suspect anything if she was a part of the caravan that took care of his flocks. Meeting him down the road (or "off the road") somewhere with a veil over her face would be extremely questionable. As we said earlier, in Middle Eastern culture this suggests a prostitute. Solomon demonstrates real concern for his lover's character and needs by giving specific directions to her as to when and how they should meet together.

He restored her confidence.

Solomon understands her insecurity and is trying to encourage her. She said, "I am dark, but lovely," and he responds by comparing her to his prize filly. Horses are animals of great beauty. A simple study of them or attendance at a professional horse show will make a big impression on you as you see the beauty, grace, and dignity of horses.

Solomon restores her confidence by calling her "my love," which is used nine times throughout the book and means "to guard" or "to care for." He has become her guardian and is promising to take care of her. This in itself is an important point in his encouragement to her.

When he compares her to his prize mare, there is much more here than the simple beauty of a well-bred horse. Notice what he says:

> *I have compared you, my love, to my filly among Pharaoh's chariots.*

In ancient Egypt, mares were never used to draw chariots —only stallions. The Hebrew text here is feminine singular, and pictures a mare loose among the royal stallions, causing intense excitement! What Solomon is saying is that Abishag is so beautiful (no matter what she felt about herself) that she causes other men to take notice immediately that here is one gorgeous woman!

Horses were decorated in ancient times, as is also done today at horse shows around the world. Solomon uses this fact in 1:10 to encourage Abishag about her "country" appearance. He will take care of that problem as well:

> *Your cheeks are lovely with ornaments,*
> *your neck with chains of gold.*

Some believe that he is referring to bridal jewels with which her natural beauty would be enhanced. Others feel that he is saying she doesn't need them because her natural beauty already compares with the beauty of a decorated horse in Pharaoh's collection.

He resolved her problem (about her appearance).

Once again we have the problem of who is speaking in this verse. Is it the daughters of Jerusalem, or is it Solomon, or perhaps both?

> *We will make you ornaments*
> *of gold with studs of silver.*

Carole and I believe that this comes from the daughters of Jerusalem under Solomon's orders. He instructs them to provide the necessary bridal jewels or queenly jewels that would identify her publicly as his queen and wife.

All of these words are encouraging to Abishag. She is being courted by Solomon and is convinced that she will make a lovely bride. No doubt about it—he wants her! He will do whatever is necessary to receive her hand in marriage.

Encouragement is a sweet word, and the Bible speaks of it often. Wives especially need it (husbands also!). What really makes wives beautiful comes from the heart of their own husbands. This may be a difficult lesson to learn if you are a married man, but it is crucially important!

3 | Say It With Love!

SONG OF SOLOMON • 1:12–2:3

She is so encouraged and stimulated by his romantic words and loving concern for how she feels that she can't wait to stir his heart by telling him how much she longs for his love and sweetness.

Chuck was basically a good man, but the way he talked to his wife left much to be desired. She frequently had periods of depression because of things he would say to her. Like so many husbands, he failed to understand the power of his words upon the spirit and attitudes of his wife. When he was confronted about this problem by several people, he always defended himself by saying, "I always speak what I feel. If she doesn't like it, then she really doesn't like me!"

He was a little surprised when a Christian friend, after hearing his typical reply, responded, "If you talked to me like that, I wouldn't like you either!" The discussion continued, and Chuck seemed to listen this time. The truth was that his wife, Ruth, did not like him at all because of the way he talked to her. He could not open his mouth without being critical. He took pride in his blunt way of speaking, which was quite rude and at times even vulgar.

Chuck finally went for help. A Christian counselor caused him to see the danger toward the emotional health of his wife: He was literally destroying her by his words. Fortunately for this couple, Chuck changed his vocabulary and learned to speak with love.

TABLE TALK

The scene facing us in this section of the Song of Solomon is "at his table" (1:12). Is this a regular meal? Some think so; others disagree. It could be describing the wedding feast, or perhaps a festive banquet announcing the engagement. The actual wedding is not found until chapter 3. Beginning in 2:8 there is a flashback or replay of their courtship days. It is possible that from 1:2 to 2:7 we have a general summary of falling in love that culminates in their sexual union on their wedding night. Then the Song backs up to tell more details about how they came together and what they experienced in their marriage.

It is not easy to answer all the problems of interpretation, but knowing the Bible's standards of morality and comparing it with the sensuality of the early verses of chapter 2 (which seem to suggest a sexual involvement by these two lovers), Carole and I believe that this is a brief look at their wedding banquet and their sexual union which followed. The Song will then back up and fill in the details of how they met and fell in love.

She describes how much he means to her.

What wonderful occasions weddings are! They are times of joy and celebration. Weddings today are accompanied by banquets and dinners at which relatives and friends can rejoice with the bride and bridegroom.

Often I have observed the wedding couple at these occasions and can see their desire for each other in the way they look at each other. It's always so special to observe this! When couples do not reflect such joyful anticipation of each other's love, I usually question what is really going on in their hearts. It's natural to feel great romance on your wedding day!

Abishag is so honored to be at Solomon's table. She refers to him as "king," and so he was. What a privilege for her to be honored publicly as his bride and queen! She couldn't resist speaking about him from her heart. Consider carefully her words of love:

*While the king is at his table, my spikenard sends
forth its fragrance. A bundle of myrrh is my beloved
to me, that lies all night between my breasts.
My beloved is to me a cluster of henna blooms
in the vineyards of En Gedi.*

She wants to please him.

She indicates her great desire to please the love of her heart:

My spikenard sends forth its fragrance.

The word translated "spikenard" speaks of costly and exotic fragrances. This is no cheap stuff from the local general store. She put on the best perfume she could find so that he would be enchanted and pleased by even the smell of her beauty!

We are reminded from this incident of how believers (the bride of Jesus Christ) should be a sweet smell in the nostrils of our Savior, the Bridegroom and Lover of our souls (cf. 2 Corinthians 2:14-16; Ephesians 5:2; Philippians 4:18). Our constant desire should be to please the Lord in all we say and do.

From what we read in this romantic love song, smells are important. We may joke about it, but couples who desire to attract and please each other need to be careful about how they smell. Love is willing to admit bad breath and do something about it. Love understands that your partner deserves something more than the odor from body sweat!

She wants to picture him as an intimate lover and friend!

When she says that Solomon is a "bundle of myrrh," she is regarding him as something very special. Myrrh was used in the holy oil of the tabernacle ceremonies (Exodus 30:23-33) and was a special fragrance for embalming (John 19:39).

The culture of Abishag's day included the wearing of a small bag of myrrh around the neck of a woman. It would have a tendency throughout the day of giving off a sweet smell to all who would come close. Abishag pictures Solomon like that bag of myrrh around her neck—close to her heart and sweet to her nostrils.

She adds, "that lies all night between my breasts." A beautiful and romantic way of putting it! That bag around the neck usually hung between the breasts of a woman. She pictures Solomon sweetly laying his head between her breasts, and she wants him to know how precious that thought is to her by describing him as a "bundle [bag] of myrrh."

Any wife who wants her husband to respond lovingly to her should communicate the romance which Abishag demonstrates in this passage. Do not pass it off as romantic foolishness. Men are attracted greatly by such romantic talk. Abishag desires Solomon's closeness and intimacy. Do you want this from your husband? Do you desire this with your wife? Then say it with love!

She wants to praise him.

Twice she calls Solomon "my beloved." The word refers to a sexual and romantic lover as well as an intimate friend.

Her second usage of it precedes a description that honors him as the best of them all:

My beloved is to me a cluster of henna blooms in the vineyards of En Gedi.

Some interpreters believe that this refers to a shrub whose leaves when crushed produce a yellow dye used in coloring hair or fingernails. The picture of such a cluster would be unusual in the midst of vineyards. The point is that Solomon stands out among all the rest. The vineyards of En Gedi were known for their quality. The whole picture here is emphasizing how special Solomon is: He is like an oasis in the desert.

Exotic spices and plants also grown in En Gedi were manufactured into cosmetics and perfumes. It is hard to tell the specific impact of her words as it relates to the meaning of "henna blooms" and "vineyards of En Gedi," but the general idea is Solomon's uniqueness. He is one in a million, and she wants him to know it!

Remind yourself that she is saying this at the wedding banquet in their honor. We have no way of knowing whether she said this to the daughters of Jerusalem or other guests at the wedding, but we suspect that she directed these words to Solomon alone. Others may have heard them, but she would care little about what they think—she is in love with this man! She adores him, and continues to praise him.

We were guests at a friend's house for dinner, and several other couples were invited. While partaking of appetizers in the living room of that home, Carole leaned over and whispered in my ear, "You are the most handsome man in this room!" I was flattered. However, I did take a quick look around, and was not overly impressed with the appearance of the other men! She sensed what I was feeling, and said once more, "You are the best in the whole world!" I really didn't

care what anyone else thought about what she said—I found
it hard to concentrate that evening!

He declares how beautiful she is!

After hearing her romantic words, he quickly responds
by saying:

> *Behold, you are fair, my love! Behold,*
> *you are fair! You have dove's eyes.*

The word "fair" is again the word "beautiful." He said
it twice so she would really know how convinced he was of
her beauty. When he said "my love," he once again reminded
her of her special place in his heart. The New International
Version of the Bible renders this "my darling."

After her words to him (1:12-14), he chose to reflect upon
what she had said and how it affected him. He spoke of her
eyes, the gateway into the soul, and said:

> *You have dove's eyes.*

The dove is faithful to its mate all its life. Solomon saw
loyalty and fidelity in her eyes, and it greatly attracted him
(as it should every husband). The dove is a symbol of peace
and purity, but it was her commitment to him alone that
allured his romantic heart to express how beautiful she was
to him.

She directs his attention to their surroundings.

His words filled her heart with greater love and joy as
she anticipated her role as his wife and queen. She comments
on the beauty of Solomon and the surroundings he had
provided for her. It was a custom to build a special bedroom
for the bride. She refers to it, and lets him know how wonderful it is and how much she wants to share it with him.

> *Behold, you are handsome, my beloved!*
> *Yes, pleasant! Also our bed is green. The beams of*

our houses are cedar, and our rafters of fir.

What makes a bedroom is not the furniture, wallpaper, pictures, or plants—it is the beauty of romantic love between those who share that sacred place!

Abishag started her words by calling him "handsome." It is the same word as the previous verse (1:15) when he called her "fair" or "beautiful." The only grammatical change is the gender. She saw *him* as beautiful. She referred not only to his appearance but also to his attitudes when she said that he was "pleasant." This man was not only a delight to look at but a pleasure to be with!

We hear it said of some women, "Their beauty is only skin deep." That can also be said of some men. They may be "hunks," as one teenager said to me when describing a boy she liked, but more is needed to experience the romance of this song! A man may be handsome in appearance, but real attractiveness in the bedroom is found in the heart—the attitudes of that man toward his wife.

What do you think about your bed?

Abishag referred to their bed as "green." It doesn't mean that they were into green colors in contrast to blues or browns! The word pictures healthy growth, and is a term referring to plants. The word "bed" means "to cover" and may picture a canopy. Some believe that these words reveal an outdoor setting (which Abishag may have preferred). It is more natural to take the words as descriptions of the bridal chamber where she was expecting to culminate their marriage by becoming one with Solomon sexually.

The beams and rafters of the bridal chamber were made from the finest woods—cedar and fir. The quality and beauty of that place was on her mind, a fitting tribute to the love they shared.

Bedrooms ought to be special places. Husbands and wives should relish their times there and look forward to relaxing and loving in that environment. It certainly is no place for an office! For a few months I put a desk, chair, books, and typewriter in our bedroom. What a bad mistake, and what a relief when I removed those items and stopped working in the bedroom!

After Abishag directed Solomon's thoughts to that special bridal chamber, she could not resist a reference to herself:

> *I am the rose of Sharon,*
> *and the lily of the valleys.*

Unfortunately, some Christian songs have used these words as though they were spoken of Solomon. By way of typology, some music makes them refer to the loveliness of our Lord Jesus Christ. The intent of such symbolism is worthy of commendation, but the accuracy is lacking. These words are spoken by Abishag about herself.

The "rose" comes from a Hebrew word meaning "to form bulbs." It could refer to a narcissus, iris, or daffodil, but certainly not a rose as we know it today. The word "Sharon" probably does not refer to the well-known plain in Israel on the Mediterranean, but rather to the region around Mount Tabor, south of the Sea of Galilee, a territory familiar to Abishag. The "lily of the valleys" picture adds some insight to the "rose of Sharon" description. Abishag is referring to herself as a simple wildflower growing in the fields. She seems to be expressing her amazement that Solomon would take her as his bride and surround her with such a beautiful bridal chamber. After all, she's just a wildflower from the fields!

He discerns her need for reassurance.

Solomon immediately responds to what she said and the insecurity she was feeling:

> *Like a lily among thorns,*
> *so is my love among the daughters.*

Her humility is obvious, but to Solomon she is something very special. He takes her reference of being merely a "lily" (not like our lily) or a wildflower of the field, and says that if this is so, then other women are thorns by comparison. What a special way of responding to her! What love flows from his mouth!

He again calls her "my love" and sets her apart from the ladies of the court. They don't deserve to be mentioned in the same breath with her. She is Solomon's "love," his intimate friend and lover. The "pretties" of the palace are nothing but "thorns" to him.

She delights in his love.

She is so encouraged and stimulated by his romantic words and loving concern for how she feels that she can't wait to stir his heart by telling him how much she longs for his love and sweetness.

It is very striking that the woman speaks as much as she does in this romantic song. Out of 117 verses, 55 are clearly from her lips and another 19 are probably her words. That is very unusual in terms of ancient love poems and songs. It tells us that it is the responsibility of the wife as well as the husband to be romantic and to say it with love.

Her words are meant to tell Solomon how much he affects her:

> *Like an apple tree among the trees of*
> *the woods, so is my beloved among the sons.*

The "apple tree" was an erotic symbol in ancient times. The "woods" speak of uncultivated, wild, and rugged forests. Solomon was contrasted with other men, but it was no competition—he won "hands down." When Abishag looked at him, she saw a romantic lover unequaled and so very desirable. She couldn't wait to experience his sexual love.

She was attracted by two special things as she compared him to an apple tree:

1. His *shade*: "I sat down in his shade with great delight."
2. His *sweetness*: "His fruit was sweet to my taste."

The shade of an apple tree could picture his protection, but more likely relief from the heat of the sun. Solomon was refreshing to her. He was like relaxing under the shade of a tree and experiencing relief. What a beautiful way of describing her lover! Wives, do you feel that way about your husbands? Do you think of them with such erotic symbolism? They would certainly be excited if you did!

The word for "taste" refers to the mouth, including the lips, teeth, tongue, etc. The Hebrew word is used of anointing a child's lips with honey in order to stimulate or motivate him. It comes to mean a method of instruction as well as a picture of dedication. It may indicate that she is attracted by how he will instruct her in the ways of love. Whatever the intricate details intended, the overall point is that of the sweetness of his love and romance. She delighted in it and in him!

Dan and Cheryl struggled a great deal in their marriage. They were both in need of romance but somewhat afraid to express it. It came out in our conversation one day at my office. Cheryl confessed that she did not relate to Dan as a romantic lover, and he felt the same way about her. They both assured me that they were committed to their marriage and were willing to do whatever was necessary to build their love and romance to the standards of the Bible. When I referred to the Song of Solomon, they both seemed surprised. (I am constantly amazed at the reluctance of couples to consult this marvelous book!)

After a few minutes of sharing the message of the Song of Solomon, both of them agreed to spend some time working on their relationship. A few weeks later I saw them at church, and she said to me, "Pastor, my husband is one delicious apple tree!" I don't get embarrassed easily, but that one did the trick!

The most important lesson to learn from the events and words shared at Solomon's "table" so long ago is that we need to be romantic in the way we communicate. Learn to say it with love!

4 | The Need for Apples and Cakes of Raisins

Face to face he communicates his love for her
by what he says and how he looks at her.
His loving patience and desire to arouse his wife
as well as himself is evident in this expression.
This is a tender and compassionate lover who wants
his wife to enjoy the experience as well.

Does food turn you on? Some people feel sexual desire by looking at certain foods (especially fruits), and others get excited by eating! Sometimes a certain food is associated with a pleasant sexual experience. Perhaps you and your spouse enjoy eating in bed, and what you eat together or feed each other makes you think warm thoughts toward your partner.

Carole and I enjoy frozen yogurt from a special place near our house. We like to slowly taste that delicious stuff while lying in bed, and other couples tell us similar stories.

Solomon and Abishag were into apples and raisin cakes. So was the entire ancient world, for these were erotic symbols and reminded people of sexual desire. The sweetness of those items were no doubt the reason for the association.

THE DESIRE TO MAKE LOVE

Verses 4-7 in chapter 2 contain a brief summary of their wedding-night experience which will be discussed in more detail later on in the book. It is approached from the wife's point of view. Abishag has been drawn romantically to Solomon and is now expressing her desire to make love to him.

The majority of husbands get really excited when they know that their wives are romantically aroused by them and truly desire to make love. When the wife never wants such sexual experience, it is a real turnoff to the husband.

Alex talked one day about his growing disappointment with Betty. He loved her, but was never really sure that she wanted him. He did not seem to doubt her love for him, but he spoke of it in rather platonic terms. He frankly asked if it was wrong for a husband to expect his wife to want sex. Alex's question is one which many husbands have experienced. There are times and temperaments which do not seem to require great sexual interest and arousal on the part of husbands and wives. A little understanding and patience goes a long way.

After further conversation with both Alex and Betty, it was obvious that Alex's attitudes were deeply affecting his wife, though he was unaware of them. When Alex changed the way he spoke and acted, Betty changed.

We couldn't help but compare Alex's problem with the romantic attitudes and kindness of King Solomon. No wonder Abishag was attracted to this man! He loved her and spoke with appreciation for her appearance and character. His compliments drew her to him.

But the other side of the story is reflected often. It is possible for wives to miss the need of their husbands for their sexual love and aggressiveness. Husbands need to be desired by their wives just as wives need their husbands to desire them. It is not wrong for the wife to desire sex with her husband. She is not simply a tool for him to use to satisfy his needs, but she has a right to sexual enjoyment and satisfaction as well. The truth is that the husband needs to know that his wife desires to make love with him!

Abishag gives three reasons why she is so motivated to make love with Solomon. The anticipation of marriage alone can be enough stimulation, but she also makes quite clear what she is feeling.

She is motivated by his loving protection.

> *He brought me to the banqueting house,*
> *and his banner over me was love.*

"The banqueting house" is literally "the house of wine." It speaks of celebration and joy. It is a common reference to the bridal chamber, where husband and wife experience sexual love.

Banners were sometimes used when an army was assembling for battle. Various companies or divisions within the army would have a banner which would help their members locate where they should be. In this respect a banner was something to look at in order to find your place. Some Bible teachers believe that this could be the point here. She would be referring to his look of love. It would be as though she were saying, "Every time he looks at me, I see love in his eyes!"

The banner can also picture a victory that has been won: It is a banner of triumph; the ones you conquered are now your possession. This is a possible picture as well.

Perhaps the simplest idea is that she finds herself under his banner of protection as well as possession. She has found her place—under the banner of Solomon—and it is a banner of love. She senses security and protection because of his love. Being under his care in the bridal chamber was not threatening to her security; it rather motivated her to make love with him. She trusted his loving care completely. She had no fears or inhibitions when thinking of Solomon's sexual lovemaking.

In a premarital counseling session of a few years ago, the petite bride-to-be expressed some concerns about the sexual aggressiveness of her prospective bridegroom. It seems that he had become sexually difficult in the months previous to their engagement, and she found it hard to keep his hands off her.

After their engagement, he became worse in his aggressiveness, very rarely caring about how she felt. She was afraid of him. He was a football player, twice her size! When she would object to his sexual advances, pleading with him to wait until marriage, he would ignore her pleas and literally attack her. With some tears she spoke of the fact that they had already had sex a number of times, that it frankly was not an enjoyable experience to her, and that she was quite afraid of what would happen after they were married.

When he was finally confronted about this he became angry and defensive, and decided to break the engagement. Later we find out that he had a few other girlfriends on the side!

When love is controlling a man's sexual desires, there is tenderness and gentleness in his heart. Restraint is always present, as well as concern for the other person's feelings and needs. A godly love is always committed to biblical standards. It's a love that you can trust. Its banner is love!

She is motivated by her strong passion.

> *Sustain me with cakes of raisins,*
> *refresh me with apples, for I am lovesick.*

Abishag is in love! Her passion is now taking over. She can hardly wait to feel his touch and to experience the joy of his sexual love for her.

The raisin and the apple, because of their sweetness, are erotic symbols. They suggest that this lovesick girl can only be rescued from her sexual passion by the embraces and kisses of her lover. When a wife experiences this kind of passion, the husband is indeed rewarded!

She used the words "sustain me" and "refresh me." It sounds selfish, but within the context of marital love it is perfectly legitimate for the wife to experience such powerful desire. The question is, will the husband be able to sustain and refresh such a wife? Many men are too selfish in their sexual lovemaking to allow this kind of scene to develop. Husbands need to be patient and loving toward their wives. Wives are not aroused as quickly, but when they do experience such passion, it is a wonderful thing for the husband to behold. He will be rewarded if he is patient, loving, and kind toward her needs. After all, according to Ephesians 5:25-33, husbands are to reflect the love of Jesus Christ toward their wives. It means that they are willing to sacrifice personal desires and needs in order to please and satisfy their wives.

Several years ago a friend shared with us that his wife was, in his words, "a sex maniac." We tried not to laugh, but it seemed funny to us when he said it. She did not seem to be that kind of person. After more conversation (and we calmed down), we realized that he was serious.

His wife had tremendous desires for sex that he was seemingly not able to fulfill. We challenged him about his duty to do so, according to 1 Corinthians 7:3. He seemed surprised. He answered, "But what if I don't feel such desire myself?" We responded, "It's still your duty." That's the bottom line. We are accountable to God and His plan for marriage, and not to our own personal feelings or desires. It is rare (but blessed!) when both husband and wife experience strong sexual passion and desire at the same time. Regardless, each spouse is responsible before God to meet the sexual needs of the other.

She is motivated by his sexual practices.

His left hand is under my head,
and his right hand embraces me.

This is not a formula or suggested position. This does not mean that a man's right hand could not be placed under a woman's head or that a left hand could not do some embracing!

While it is poetic, it is also quite sensual. The word "embrace" is from a Hebrew word which can mean "to fondle" or even "to stimulate sexually."

The picture here is of the husband and wife lying in bed together. With his left hand he draws her close to him facially, and with his right hand he stimulates her sexually. Face to face he communicates his love for her by what he says and how he looks at her. His loving patience and desire to arouse his wife as well as himself is evident in this expression. This is a tender and compassionate lover who wants his wife to enjoy the experience as well. Though he is motivated quickly by the sight or touch of her, he is well aware that she needs time and patient moments of preparation in order to feel strong passion and response toward him.

There are multitudes of books (both secular and Christian) that you can read on the subject of sex. Some are good, and some are not so good. Couples planning to get married do not have to feel unprepared because they have not studied all these books. God's love controlling our hearts is sufficient preparation. The joy of discovery is a precious experience that no couple should be deprived of before they are married.

The best preparation for sexual lovemaking in marriage is found here in the Song of Solomon. Though poetic and exceedingly romantic, it gives specific help to all who need advice on sexual love. It encourages young husbands to be loving, patient, and concerned about their wives and the needs they have

A CRUCIAL COMMAND

Song of Solomon 2:7 is repeated two more times in this romantic poem, in 3:5 and 8:4. It is something like a refrain, but it is also more than that. It carries a powerful and profound message to all who would enjoy sex the way God intended. It is a defense of marital love. It is a statement that warns against premarital or extramarital sex.

I charge you, O daughters of Jerusalem,
by the gazelles or by the does of the field, do
not stir up nor awaken love until it pleases.

The gazelles and does are dropped out of the passage in 8:4, but the major emphasis remains the same. The command is given to the ladies of the court, probably virgins, that they be careful about arousing sexual passion.

Do not stir up nor awaken love until it pleases.

Don't arouse yourself or someone else sexually until it is time for that passion to be satisfied. We believe that this love song from God through His servant Solomon is consistent with the teaching of Scripture concerning sex. Premarital and extramarital sex are forbidden. Consider the following:

Exodus 20:14: Prohibits adultery.
Leviticus 18:6-23 and 20:10-21: Condemns incest, adultery, homosexuality, and bestiality.
Proverbs 5:15-23 and 6:24-35: Condemns extramarital sex (adultery and prostitution).
Romans 1:24-32: Condemns homosexuality and all kinds of sexual immorality.
Romans 13:13: Condemns sexual immorality.

1 Corinthians 5:1-13: Condemns incest and all kinds of sexual immorality.

1 Corinthians 6:9,10; Galatians 5:19-21; Ephesians 5:3-5; Colossians 3:5,6; Revelation 21:8; 22:15: Condemn sexual immorality and warn that its continual practice reveals that you are not saved!

Many more passages could be used, but these will suffice to show us the Bible's view of premarital or extramarital sex. The only kind of sex honored in the Bible is that which occurs within marriage. Read carefully this important verse:

*Marriage is honorable among all, and
the bed undefiled; but fornicators and adulterers
God will judge.*

You may not agree with what the Bible teaches, but there is no margin for misinterpretation as to what the Bible is actually saying: It condemns all kinds of sexual involvement outside of marriage, but honors it within marriage.

COMMITMENT AND TRUST

We believe that Song of Solomon 2:7, 3:5, and 8:4 are poetic words agreeing with the Bible's standards of morality. Some translations render the phrase "until *it* pleases" as "until *he* pleases." This would leave the matter in the hands of the male lover. Whenever he is ready, that's when it's okay to make love! We simply do not believe that this is the point of these verses. We believe that the phrase applies to sexual love ("do not stir up nor awaken *love*") and not the male sexual lover. The time indicated by the words "it pleases" is marriage, as indicated by the teaching of this romantic love song.

Upon close scrutiny of the content of this song we find

several reasons for warning against premarital or extramarital sex. The first of these is this:

SEX OUTSIDE OF MARRIAGE CANNOT
GUARANTEE SEXUAL CELEBRATION.

It can produce guilt and frustration, but it cannot produce the kind of sexual joy and satisfaction which sex within marriage can produce. True sexual pleasure hinges on *commitment* and *trust*.

Abishag is excited with the sexual celebration awaiting her in the bridal chamber with Solomon. But she is also very much aware of the sexual passion which she feels. She can see the danger of it. It would be quite easy to lose control. Sexual passion is often uncontrollable when it is allowed to exist outside the boundaries of biblical commitment in marriage. Abishag realizes this at the moment of her intense passion and desire for Solomon's love, and thus warns the ladies of the court.

THE JOYOUS BOND OF MARRIAGE

There is a sense in which people involved in premarital or extramarital sex do experience excitement and a measure of fulfillment in the sheer act of making love or having sex. The problem is that without commitment to each other in marriage, the experience cannot guarantee that one's emotions will be rewarded with what took place. People often feel empty, lonely, and unfulfilled even when sexual involvement has just taken place.

Another important factor deals with responsibility or accountability to the personality and needs of the other person. Without marital commitment, there is no guarantee. People often feel used even though they enjoyed the tie involved in making love. It almost seems a paradox. How can something so enjoyable fail to bring lasting joy and peace?

The sexual celebration and joy of which the Bible speaks cannot occur without marriage. However, marriage does not guarantee that it will occur, either. We all need to depend upon the love of God and power of the Holy Spirit. Just because a couple is married and lives under the same roof is no guarantee that true sexual celebration and joy is taking place in that home.

Apples and cakes of raisins symbolize the intensity of Abishag's sexual passion and desire to make love with Solomon, but the only way this can bring lasting fulfillment and joy is within the bond of marriage!

5 | *Where Are the Gazelles?*

SONG OF SOLOMON • 2:8-17

Commitment is the most important ingredient cementing two people in marriage. It is a quality that can be observed even before the marriage takes place. It usually involves two things: protection of the relationship and loyalty to the relationship.

After a brief look at the love relationship and marriage of Solomon and Abishag, we are taken back to their courtship days. Abishag reviews in her mind and heart the beauty of those days when Solomon came to her home to win her heart.

The thoughts of this passage continue until 3:5, where Abishag again warns the ladies of the court about premarital sex. Her emphasis here is on the fact that premarital sex hinders your objectivity in making the correct choice of a life partner.

Song of Solomon 3:6 launches into the wedding ceremony and a marvelous bridal procession. But, as in every wedding, there are many experiences which must come before the marriage.

After preaching a series of messages on the Song of Solomon we were inundated with notes, cards, and letters about romantic love and marriage relationships. Much of this was given to us by singles who were interested in marriage. One of the messages was entitled "Where Are the Gazelles?" and dealt with the kind of man which single girls are looking for. A couple of single girls in our church took a trip to Colorado, and from there mailed us a postcard with a striking mountain scene and a beautiful deer. They wrote, "We had to come to Colorado to find a gazelle!"

WHAT IS A GAZELLE?

A gazelle looks like a deer, runs swiftly, and is most graceful. In Song of Solomon the gazelle is mentioned seven times. In referring to Solomon it is used with the words "young stag" (2:9,17; 8:14), and no doubt implies a full-grown gazelle in the prime of its life and strength. In referring to the breasts of Abishag, Solomon compares them to "two fawns, twins of a gazelle" (4:5 and 7:3), which refers to gazelles before they are full-grown, when they are soft, gentle, and desirable to caress.

In ancient times the gazelle was a symbol of sexual virility, and was a most complimentary term. This comparison of Abishag is much like Solomon's reference to her in 1:9 when he said, "I have compared you, my love, to my filly among Pharaoh's chariots." She is the "filly," and he is the "gazelle"!

ENTHUSIASTIC ABOUT HIS COMING

The voice of my beloved! Behold, he comes leaping upon the mountains, skipping upon the hills. My beloved is like a gazelle or a young stag. Behold, he stands behind our wall; he is looking through the windows, gazing through the lattice.

There is nothing like the enthusiasm of that first date when it's someone special with whom you have already fallen in love! You wonder about the feelings of the other person: Will he or she respond to me according to my hopes?

It was a rare occasion when a mighty king like Solomon would visit one of the farming villages in the north. But it was even more rare for such a king to go that far for a date! He could easily have commanded his troops to get any woman he wanted. The fact that he actually came to her home contains a wealth of information about Solomon and the love he had for Abishag.

Abishag is enthused because of two basic things: the words he speaks, and the way he comes to her. Her opening words are "the voice of my beloved." When you are in love, the mere sound of your lover's voice is sweet music to your ear!

Every husband and wife should evaluate the way he and she communicate to each other. Does the sound of your spouse's voice seem like beautiful music to your ear, or is it like the clanging of cymbals or a discordant note? There is tremendous help for us in 1 Corinthians 13, the love chapter of the Bible. It helps us understand why we may not sound so good to our marital partner. Through the help of the Lord we can all learn to speak more beautifully and romantically to each other.

Abishag is also enthusiastic about the way he comes to her. He is not taking his time, slowly approaching as if to say, "Why did I come all this way to meet her?" Verse 8 says that he is "leaping upon the mountains, skipping upon the hills." Who is this? King Solomon!

Verse 9 does not imply a "Peeping Tom" as Solomon looks through the windows. In ancient dwellings with courtyards, this was easy to do and was expected. It is not a quick glance, either—he is taking his time looking for her and at her, and it is a look of love and excitement. The king of Israel has come all this way to date the love of his heart, and he comes with excitement and enthusiasm. He can hardly wait to cast his eyes upon this lovely creature. And of course this causes Abishag to be thrilled with anticipation over the date.

THE PURPOSE OF DATING

Not all cultures handle dating the same way. American dating is often different from other forms in terms of romance and freedoms. Parental decisions are usually not critical, and family responsibilities are rarely considered. The meaningful word to Americans is the word *romance*. We are looking for someone whom we can love and who in return will love us.

Counselors disagree as to the ideal length of courtship, but most encourage a couple to take enough time to know each other well. Preventing a possible divorce in the future is often the reason behind the advice for a longer dating period.

Bob and Debbie were in love, or at least that's what they said to many of their friends. They had been dating for three weeks and now decided that they wanted to be married. We suggested that they take more time, but they were insulted at the idea. They were very upset when we tried to warn them about short courtships ending in divorce. They were different, or so they said. These two teenagers got married in spite of many people who counseled them to wait. One year later they were divorced. It happens too often.

1. *Dating is a time to know each other well without sexual involvement.*

Sex confuses things. You cannot be objective about a person once you become sexually involved. Dating is a time to learn all you can about a person's habits, friends, goals, family, character, etc. You will learn much about how you will be treated later on in marriage by the way you are treated in a long courtship. Short ones usually reveal very little in this regard. You are taking a big chance, and you may lose!

2. *Dating is a time to evaluate your compatibility and sense of responsibility.*

Even though "opposites attract," it is important to know how flexible and compatible you are with each other, especially in areas of disagreement or difference. What kind of responsibility do you feel toward the other person's life and needs? Do you really care for him or her, and are you willing to pay the costs involved in marriage? It will mean real sacrifice in the areas of time, personal interests, and financial resources.

3. *Dating is a time to understand the depth of your love and commitment to each other.*

Some people "fall in love" quickly, but most of us "grow in love" gradually. Time reveals a great deal about the depth of our relationships. *Commitment* is the foundation of a good marriage—not sex or "falling in love." When you speak those wedding vows, God expects you to keep them. They are "till death do us part." (See Romans 7:1-3 and 1 Corinthians 7:39.)

ENTICED BY HIS COMPANIONSHIP

A card in a local bookstore reads on the front, "All we need is. . ." and then the inside prints out ". . .to be together!" Couples who love each other are enticed by being together. They are not irritated in each other's presence. They feel that no one on earth is more desirable as a friend than their marital partner!

Now notice how Solomon handled his date with Abishag. *He extended an invitation.*

Rise up, my love, my fair one, and come away.

This may not be the way your first date began, but you

have to admit that it's a great approach! Solomon repeats those words at the end of verse 13.

We realize that girls are calling boys today for dates; it's a part of our cultural perspective. But Carole and I think the boys should be the ones doing the inviting. Initiative in love and marriage should rest primarily on the shoulders of the husband. God holds him accountable for what takes place in that marriage and family. It may seem like a small point, but we prefer the boys to take the initiative. Be patient, girls!

He explained the timing.

These poetic phrases are romantic statements about the timing in which the love of Solomon and Abishag is being experienced. They express facts about what is past ("the winter") and gone ("the rain") and what has come ("flowers" and "the time of singing"). It appears that the timing of this courtship was placed in the spring, when a young man's fancy truly turns to love!

It is a time to sing and rejoice for this couple. They are falling in love, and all nature joins them in celebrating. Solomon also makes reference to the timing by referring to the approaching harvest of figs and grapes. In 2:13 he says two things that would have especially touched the heart of this country girl who had spent most of her life working in the vineyards:

1. The fig tree puts forth her green figs.
2. The vines with the tender grapes give a good smell.

Figs and grapes are like the apples and cakes of raisins we mentioned earlier. They were erotic symbols, picturing the blossoming of love. Solomon is saying that the time for love has come. Spring is in the air, and the smells of delicious fruit have stimulated his nostrils for the smell and joy of being with his love, Abishag.

He expressed his desires.

*O my dove, in the clefts of the rock, in the secret
places of the cliff, let me see your countenance, let me
hear your voice; for your voice is sweet, and your
countenance is lovely.*

When Carole reads these lines, she sort of swoons a little!
I have to admit that this man Solomon is smooth with the
words! Notice what he calls her: "my dove." In 2:10 he opened
with "my love, my fair one." The dove was a symbol of purity
and gentleness, with the emphasis here upon gentleness. It
is the dove "in the clefts of the rock." In addition to the fact
that doves resorted to such a place for security and protection, Solomon may be thinking that this beautiful woman has
been hidden away, like a dove in the clefts of the rock. It pictures her simplicity and remoteness from the world around
her. Solomon knows he has found a hidden treasure!

In his communication to her, he speaks of two things: her
countenance (appearance) and her voice. The one is "lovely"
and the other is "sweet." The word for "voice" in 2:14 is the
same as in 2:12, where he referred to the "voice of the turtle-
dove." That bird has a soft, gentle, cooing sound that is quite
enchanting.

Small wonder that Abishag is enticed by the companionship of Solomon! All his ways and words are sweet and romantic. He does not barge in and demand his own way and rights;
he is gentle and loving, and in the end quite persuasive.

COMMITMENT AND PROTECTION

*Catch us the foxes, the little foxes that spoil
the vines, for our vines have tender grapes.*

*My beloved is mine, and I am his. He feeds his flock
among the lilies.*

Commitment is the most important ingredient cementing two people in marriage. It is a quality that can be observed even before the marriage takes place. It usually involves two things: protection of the relationship and loyalty to the relationship.

The phrase "catch us the foxes" can also be translated "let us catch," and this fits better: It is a mutual decision to protect their relationship.

The picture of little foxes that can damage vines with tender grapes is most graphic and would be quite meaningful to Abishag, who had worked in the vineyards and experienced this frequently. There are many such "little foxes" that can hurt a marriage, and this couple is determined to deal with those matters before they get married.

Their love relationship is compared with "tender grapes" that can easily be hurt by the activity of the little foxes. It pictures the need for sensitivity and concern because our love for each other is at times most fragile, and can be damaged easily by critical words, false suspicions, selfishness, flirtations, etc.

Ron said he loved Roberta very much, but his actions were not very convincing to her. In every social setting to which their dating would take them, he would be flirting with every girl there. She would speak to him about this, but he would simply laugh at her and say that it didn't mean anything. A red flag was now in her mind regarding their coming marriage. It was good she felt that way, because her suspicions proved right when she found out about his sexual exploits with other women. She ended the relationship quickly, and later found a Christian husband who today brings her much joy. The sad part of this story is that Ron has been divorced three times, and can't seem to find a permanent relationship with anyone.

ARE YOU LOYAL TO YOUR MARRIAGE?

In addition to being protective of marriage, commitment

also involved loyalty, and Abishag expresses this beautifully to Solomon in 2:16:

My beloved is mine, and I am his.

During their courtship days they committed themselves to each other. When the "engagement" was made, it was time to say goodbye to all other potential lovers, and to exercise commitment and loyalty.

Do you sense that your marital partner belongs to you and is absolutely loyal to you? This doesn't mean that we are all perfect (there will be times of failure and temptation), but it does mean that committed people have learned to say no because of the loyalty they feel toward each other. Someone else may seem quite attractive, but loyalty says no to the enticement.

When Nate got involved with another woman, he had no idea it would affect his wife the way it did. She was devastated by his disloyalty and remained in semishock for several months. She simply could not believe that after 20 years of marriage he would do such a thing. She recognized the possibility of carnality in the heart of every believer, but could not understand the fact that Nate continued this relationship over several years and expressed to this woman that he wanted her so much that he was willing to leave his wife.

Nate's wife told us, "It would have been easy to forgive him for some momentary lapse and temporary sexual involvement, but how can I forgive him for years of dishonesty and disloyalty?"

We counseled her a great deal about the meaning of forgiveness and how the Lord taught us to forgive 70 times seven. It didn't help much. She had to battle these matters in her heart. She had a right to divorce him, but we do not advise people that way. Forgiveness and restoration are always better. However, we did learn the terrible consequences of disloyalty upon the innocent partner. As it turned out, there were also terrible results in Nate's life. As he said to us, "I wish it had never happened!" But it did, and now they both suffer from it. Though they are learning to adjust, there are many moments of defeat and discouragement that arise in their hearts because of this disloyalty.

Commitment is so important to a marital relationship. We must be protective as well as loyal. Solomon and Abishag had the wisdom to talk about this aspect of marriage during their courtship.

EXCITED ABOUT THEIR COURTSHIP

Until the day breaks and the shadows flee away, turn, my beloved, and be like a gazelle or a young stag upon the mountains of Bether.

Abishag is thrilled with their courtship and cannot wait until they are together again. The last phrase of the previous verse says, "He feeds his flock among the lilies." Abishag knew that Solomon had many duties and responsibilities to fulfill as the king and shepherd of Israel. She anticipates their time together and cannot wait for his return.

The "mountains of Bether" are variously interpreted by commentators, and the exact location of such a place (if literal) is impossible to determine. The wording may be a poetic device, since that is common in this romantic love song. The word "Bether" in Hebrew means "separation." She may simply be anticipating the time when the two of them can be alone, separated from the world around them and the duties of the court. It is quite possible that she is anticipating their sexual coming together in private on the wedding night.

A FINAL WORD TO GAZELLES!

Many single men appear to be more like "bulls in a china

shop" than gazelles! Gazelles speak of gracefulness, beauty, and love. It is time for our present culture to drop the so-called "macho" image for men, and to return to biblical standards of masculinity which emphasize strength and beauty dwelling together in the same body.

It is not only a feminine trait to be soft and tender. Men need to learn how to be romantic, and God's Word offers the best help. Kindness to women is continually urged in the Scriptures. Treating them like "things" to be exploited is a violation of biblical morality and love.

Single women are looking for gazelle types—that's for sure! But married women would also like to live with a gazelle-type husband! Have your gazellelike traits deteriorated into elephantlike steps? In your attitudes toward your wife, are you more like a gorilla than a gazelle? Give this some thought and prayer!

Searching for Love

SONG OF SOLOMON • 3:1-5

*Love is so vital to any relationship if it is
to be lasting and capable of enduring
difficult situations and struggles that
inevitably come. True love is willing
to make a lifelong commitment.*

———

When a couple becomes engaged, it's time for serious evaluation and planning. The courtship period of Solomon and Abishag is described from Song of Solomon 2:8 to 3:5, and the actual wedding procession and celebration commences in 3:6-11.

Weddings are public celebrations that need to take place. Couples should have their vows confirmed before witnesses, thus making themselves accountable for the things they promise to each other.

Engagements are usually private occasions, but need not be so. In ancient times a meal was often celebrated by the couple and their relatives when the engagement was announced. Engagements could be broken only by official divorce. They were taken to be binding upon the couple.

When Carole and I got engaged, her father impressed upon me the importance of my commitment to his "little girl." He took me aside privately and said, "I'd better never hear of you hurting my girl in any way!" Since he was a former boxer and pretty fair athlete, I listened real well! He was very serious in the way he talked to me that day, and I appreciate what he said more and more as time goes on. Getting engaged is a very serious step!

IS THIS A DREAM?

These early verses in chapter 3 are interpreted in various ways by different writers. Some believe that this is not a dream but a real experience that Abishag had. We have come to believe, however, that this is simply a dream on the part of Abishag that emphasizes the importance of her commitment to Solomon and her resolve to go through with the wedding.

Verse 1 opens...

By night on my bed.

This seems to suggest a dream. But just because it's a dream does not mean that it is not to be taken seriously. The content of this dream must be important because it is placed within God's Word. Abishag learns three important things through it.

Her dream reveals the need for careful evaluation.

By night on my bed I sought the one I love;
I sought him, but I did not find him. "I will rise
now," I said, "and go about the city; in the streets
and in the squares I will seek the one I love." I
sought him, but I did not find him. The watchmen

*who go about the city found me, to whom I said, "Have
you seen the one I love?"*

The word "night" is plural in Hebrew and may suggest
that this is a recurring dream. We would say "night after
night."

The main emphasis of this recurring dream deals with
the fear of losing her lover. It suggests a good bit of insecurity
on her part, and is quite understandable considering who he
is (the king of Israel) and who she is (a simple country girl).
Twice she says, "I did not find him." A tremendous sense of
loss was gripping her heart in this dream!

THE ONE I LOVE

Four times Abishag uses the phrase "the one I love" to
describe Solomon as her lover and prospective bridegroom.
It indicates that she has begun to realize what he means to
her. This will encourage her to make a commitment in her
heart to go ahead with the marriage.

Some will ask, "Is it necessary to be in love with a person
before you get married?" A young, good-looking man asked
us that question recently. He was interested in the Christian
ministry and was thinking about becoming a pastor. He felt
that he should be married to set an example before a congre-
gation and to have the kind of experience necessary to man-
age a church. He argued this from 1 Timothy 3, and we were
not too concerned at that point.

As he continued to talk with us, however, we became
more concerned. Marriage to him was a necessity, not because
of sexual pressure or need, but because of his anticipated ministry in the future. The girl he was interested in was attractive
and sweet in her attitudes. He felt that she would make a great
pastor's wife. When we asked him if he loved her, he said,

"I'm not sure, but I don't think that is really necessary if she is willing to get married." We disagree.

While there are cultures that do matchmaking for their young people, and marriages are often arranged without romantic love, we do not believe this is based on biblical teaching. The Bible emphasizes romantic love in this Song of Solomon, and we believe that before marriage takes place, couples should be in love with each other. Love is so vital to any relationship if it is to be lasting and capable of enduring difficult situations and struggles that inevitably come. True love is willing to make a lifelong commitment, but commitments that are made in marriage without love are lacking in depth and maturity.

In her dream, Abishag is wrestling with her commitment to Solomon. Should she proceed with the wedding? Does she really love him? Is he her one and only?

A man should look at his future wife and be able to say, "She's the one I love!" A woman should be able to do the same.

I SOUGHT HIM!

In her dream, Abishag tells us four times that she is seeking the one she loves. It expresses her strong desire for him. Her dream is helping her to evaluate how much she really wants this man.

When I was dating Carole (she in college and I in graduate school), we were both on the same campus but had classes in different buildings. I would often walk outside (sometimes in subzero temperatures!) and anxiously look for her. There were other boys who had dated her, but I was *seeking* her! I went to buildings where I thought she would be and waited outside classrooms, hoping to get one glimpse of her before she went to another class. I was lovesick, but extremely excited! She was so special, and I couldn't wait until we were together again.

Abishag was sensing deeply her desire for Solomon, and it was settling her decision about marrying him. This was the one: She loved him deeply and would search the whole world for him if she had to. That's the kind of love that makes a great marriage!

Her decision requires love and loyalty.

As Abishag continues her dream, she expresses what happened when she finally found the one she loved and the one she was seeking all over the streets of the city:

> *Scarcely had I passed by them, when I found*
> *the one I love. I held him and would not*
> *let him go, until I had brought him to the*
> *house of my mother, and into the chamber*
> *of her who conceived me.*

Songs have been written about these words. One says "O Love That Will Not Let Me Go." Beautiful words! It reminds us of the original teaching of Genesis 2:24 about the bond of marriage:

> *Therefore a man shall leave his father*
> *and mother and be joined to his wife,*
> *and they shall become one flesh.*

"To be joined" to your wife is often expressed "to cleave." It indicates that those who are joined together cannot be separated. It means to glue yourself to her, and never let her go! There is a tenacity about Abishag's dream at this point that every couple needs to consider. How strongly do you want to keep the person you are married to? Or would you like to trade that person in for a newer model?

John and Cynthia had many problems, but the basic one they could not face. They wanted to talk about how different they were and how many problems they had in getting along with each other. But the real issue underneath their verbiage was the weak commitment they felt for each other. They were both interested in getting a divorce, and they both felt that someone else could make them more happy.

Lots of people think that way: Someone else could make them more happy than their present spouse. How foolish we are, for we usually take our problems with us into the next relationship!

We confronted John and Cynthia about the matter of strong commitment, a love that will not let a person go. They both confessed that they did not feel this way toward each other. Their need was to depend upon God's love to straighten them out, not to get another partner. Fortunately, they both decided to go God's way, and their marriage is thriving and strong today. They learned about the love of God that simply *will not let go!*

I HELD HIM!

In her dream, Abishag grabs Solomon and hangs on for dear life! We find this extremely important. Even when a couple embraces each other, there should be intensity in that hug which other people never experience. You may give a hug to a friend, but the hug between spouses ought to be special and strong. Hang on, and don't let go!

This hug was also bathed in the desire to make love. Abishag realizes in her dream that this is what she needed to convince her that the wedding should take place. She goes to bed with him in her dream. She desires him physically, and states that she would not let go "until I had brought him to the house of my mother, and into the chamber of her who conceived me."

This was not simply a desire to have her fiance meet her mother! The "chamber of her who conceived me" is speaking about the bedroom where her mother and father had sexual relationships that resulted in her own birth. She now dreams about bringing Solomon into that sacred place in order to make love with him in the same way, which she hopes will result in their own family.

When a couple is ready for marriage, there should be evidence of strong physical desire for each other. To be sure, mere physical desire for a person is not enough and may be deceiving; it does not mean, for example, that we should be married to every person toward whom we feel sexual desire! But a couple who plans to be married should definitely desire each other in this way.

Her desires must be controlled.

The dream of Abishag has convinced her to be married to Solomon. He is the one she loves and the one she seeks. She wants to make love with him, and in her dream she takes him to the bedroom.

Sexual desire is to be fulfilled in marriage alone; that's the teaching of the Bible. Sex outside of marriage is sin: That principle has not changed. Abishag realizes that the standards for marriage are established by God, and so in the midst of her sexual desire for Solomon she makes a statement that warns other people about trying to fulfill such desires outside of marriage (she gave these words previously in 2:7):

I charge you, O daughters of Jerusalem,
by the gazelles or by the does of the field,
do not stir up nor awaken love until it pleases.

Earlier we stated the background behind the Bible's warning about premarital or extramarital sex. We also mentioned that the phrase "until it pleases" is more correct than "until he pleases." The reference is to lovemaking, not the lover. It is dealing with the arousal of sexual passion and desire. We indicated that Song of Solomon 2:7 gives this principle:

SEX OUTSIDE OF MARRIAGE CANNOT
GUARANTEE SEXUAL CELEBRATION.

We then explained why that is so. Another principle is found in Song of Solomon 3:5 that is so important to our understanding about sex:

SEX OUTSIDE OF MARRIAGE CANNOT
GUARANTEE PERSONAL COMMITMENT.

That's what Abishag is wrestling with in her dream. Personal commitment in the heart must be settled before sexual involvement takes place. Otherwise a person cannot be objective about the person whom he or she wants to marry. You lose objectivity when you engage in sexual relationships. Your passion and desire will overpower your ability to reason with facts and draw sound conclusions.

Jack and Alicia found out the significance of this principle in their relationship. They had engaged in sex on numerous occasions and now began to conclude that marriage was for them. But because of the fact that their relationship was based on sex, they discovered little common ground or interests outside of jumping into bed. They began to argue a great deal, and felt romance only when sex took place.

Their story could be repeated many times over. Unfortunately, not many couples survive heavy sexual involvement before marriage. Research indicates that marriages that result from such heavy involvement usually are not strong, and chances for divorce increase significantly. The sexual desire often diminishes after the marriage vows are spoken, and in order to create the feeling of passion which they once experienced, the attention must be directed toward another person. Affairs often result, along with great heartache and pain.

We are so thankful for God's grace and forgiveness. If we confess and forsake our sins, there is hope. God can heal our emotions and rebuild our love for each other.

COMMITMENT: THE KEY TO GOOD MARRIAGES

When a couple decides to wait until marriage before they engage in sexual intercourse, they are building strength into their marriage. Saying no to your sexual desires is a critically important matter. These desires will not diminish when you get married, and in fact they become more important after you are married.

You must refuse to have sex with anyone other than your marital partner. Sex with someone else after you are married is still adultery: God's sexual laws have not changed, nor have the consequences changed. Decreasing sexual vitality and emotional turmoil will result for those who engage in sexual immorality. Much pain and hurt will happen to your marital partner, and it will be increasingly difficult to find sexual satisfaction with your marriage partner.

Abishag needed this dream, and so do we. Commitment is a matter of the heart first. After true love is settled within, we can speak the words without hesitation or reluctance. We enjoy lovemaking the most when there is genuine trust and commitment!

7 | Let's Get Married!

Weddings are wonderful, but as we know so well, they are only the beginning. After the wedding comes the marriage.

What beautiful occasions weddings are! We have seen many of them, and we love them all. Each couple believes that their wedding is the best one as well as the most creative.

What a moment it is when the organist or pianist plays that wedding march and the bride, with her arm on her father, begins her procession down the aisle! It's a time to celebrate, even though the parents start to cry. The bridegroom starts to get excited as he sees the woman he's been dating looking more beautiful than ever!

WHY ALL THE ATTENTION FOR THE BRIDE?

That's what one young man in a bridal party asked me

at the wedding rehearsal. He was curious as to why so much attention and planning was directed toward the bride and so little toward the bridegroom. He said, "The bride comes down the aisle with great fanfare, everyone standing as she walks and admiring her beautiful dress and appearance, while the groom, usually in a black tux, sneaks in from the side!"

According to the Bible, the focus is on the bridegroom as well as the bride. The great attraction in a spiritual marriage is the Bridegroom—our Lord Jesus Christ, to whom we believers, representing the bride, are married by faith (Matthew 25:6, Ephesians 5:22-33, Revelation 19:7-9).

Several years ago a young man about to be married decided to do something to correct this matter of focusing on the bride coming down the aisle. He had his bride come down the aisle with her father, but he wasn't at the front to meet her. The trumpet fanfare began after the bride was already at the front: The back door swung open, and down the aisle came the bridegroom in a white tuxedo!

The wedding procession and ceremony of Song of Solomon 3:6-11 focuses on the bridegroom as well as the bride. After all, Solomon is the king of Israel, the wealthiest and wisest of all the ancient monarchs. Abishag, though a country girl, was the attraction because of her beauty, but even more because of the attention and honor which Solomon gave her.

WHERE DOES THE WEDDING TAKE PLACE?

Who is this coming out of the wilderness
like pillars of smoke?

The word "wilderness" is used 270 times in the Old Testament and refers to pastureland. This is a reference to the bride's home. The engagement usually takes place in the bridegroom's home, and the wedding procession (usually a year later) starts at the bride's home and ends at the couple's new residence.

The words "Who is this?" are feminine. It refers to Abishag, the bride, or possibly to Solomon's couch mentioned in 3:7 (feminine noun). In 6:10 such an expression is applied to Abishag, and again in 8:5. So it would seem natural and logical to take these words as referring to Abishag as she sits upon a special wedding couch which Solomon has prepared for her.

The words "coming out of the wilderness" speak of contrast as Solomon sees her coming. She is obviously a gorgeous sight, and it seems quite amazing that she comes out of country life rather than from the beautiful surroundings of the palace.

HOW COME SHE SMELLS SO GOOD?

Perfumed with myrrh and frankincense,
with all the merchant's fragrant powders.

Abishag did not have these exotic fragrances available in her country surroundings. They were provided by Solomon, and were indications of his great love for her. He provided her with all the perfumes any woman could ever hope to use, and saw to it that she was marvelously prepared for this very special day.

In 1:11 we saw how Solomon promised to adorn her. Now in 3:6, we see how he fulfills that promise. No doubt he sent a caravan of people and supplies to prepare his beautiful bride for the wedding procession.

God's love is being pictured here. Solomon is like our Lord, though even with his wealth and great example he comes far short of our Savior's loving care for us. We smell good because He has made us beautiful, covering us with the fragrances of His love for us. He is the loving, caring Bridegroom, and we are the bride. The day of our wedding celebration has not yet arrived, but we wear the engagement ring of His salvation and rest in the security of His promises to us.

WHY SO MANY ATTENDANTS?

Behold, it is Solomon's couch,
with sixty valiant men around it,
of the valiant of Israel.
They all hold swords, being expert in war.
Every man has his sword on his thigh
because of fear in the night.

A wedding for the king should be a major production, more special than anyone else's wedding. People expect it, and it seems appropriate to honor this couple in a greater way than we would do for others with lesser positions in life.

The main reason for these 60 valiant men is protection. Solomon did not want anything to happen to his bride. Here is another evidence of his love for her. He was concerned about her safety and security. Every husband should feel the same. Too many men have lost the sense of their role as loving protector of the wife.

The journey from her home in the fields north of the Samaritan hills to the walls of Jerusalem was a long one, and subject to many dangers. These men were not novices, but "expert in war." They strapped their swords to their thighs and were arrayed for battle. No complacency or indifference was allowed. This was the king's bride they were to protect!

WHAT ABOUT SOLOMON'S COUCH?

It may sound strange to twentieth-century ears, but Solomon wanted his bride to be carried. He did not want her feet to be hurt and worn out by the long journey. He prepared a couch upon which she should be carried. This would immediately show to everyone how much he loved her and honored her. A country girl was used to walking through the hills and fields, but Solomon would have none of that; this was the wedding procession, and nothing was too good for his beauty!

It is also important to recognize that the couch belonged to Solomon. It was no doubt marked in special ways to make sure that every person who saw it would know that it belonged to the king. A person had better think twice before ignoring it or thinking lightly of it! One cannot help but be impressed with all that Solomon has done to demonstrate his love and respect for Abishag.

One of the great needs of our day is for husbands to honor their wives. First Peter 3:7 contains these important words:

Likewise you husbands, dwell with them
with understanding, giving honor to the wife,
as to the weaker vessel, and as being
heirs together of the grace of life,
that your prayers may not be hindered.

The Bible teaches that husbands are to give honor to their wives, and that failure to do so results in unanswered prayers.

Harry and Rebecca had lots of struggles in their 12 years of marriage. She resisted him continually, and he did not seem to enjoy her presence or her communication. He was always criticizing her in public and revealing her "many faults" to others. One day he shared with us his frustration, and said, "Frankly, I don't like the woman!"

We were not the only ones who suspected that he felt this way. It was obvious by his attitudes toward his wife and the things he said about her. We confronted him with 1 Peter 3:7 about honoring his wife, and he laughed. He said that it would be impossible for him to honor his wife until she "shaped up."

When he heard us encourage him to honor his wife because God commanded him to do so, he became nervous and defensive. He responded, "If I did that, she would get a big head!" Presumably this meant that she could not handle such honor and would become unbearably proud and conceited by all the honor he might bestow! This frankly amused us, since he had shown no respect for her in the past.

The good news is that Harry started to respond to what the Bible teaches. It was difficult for him at first. There were so many things he wanted to change in Rebecca's life. Interestingly, when he stopped trying to change her, and began to honor her for the woman she was and for the good things that she did, she started to change. Today he is thrilled with the results, and they seem to have a brand-new start in their married life together.

HERE COMES THE BRIDEGROOM!

Song of Solomon 3:9,10 pictures the bridegroom in all his glory:

> *Of the wood of Lebanon Solomon the king made himself a palanquin: He made its pillars of silver, its support of gold, its seat of purple, its interior paved with love by the daughters of Jerusalem.*

A "palanquin" is a seat or (in this case) a throne. Ancient leaders would spend a great deal of money and effort to make these seats beautiful as well as symbolic. They were often designed and carved to tell a story (usually the exploits of the king) of how great he was.

Solomon's throne was unique in that the finest wood in

the world was used—the wood of Lebanon. The strength of this unique seat was found in its "pillars of silver," which portrays a person of great wealth. The "gold" and "purple" are materials speaking of royalty and majesty, fitting for this bridegroom, the king of Israel!

In describing the throne of Solomon, we cannot resist reflecting on the throne of God and the Lamb (Jesus Christ). It is mentioned in Revelation 22:3 as a main feature of the heavenly city, in which all believers will one day gather to worship and praise the Lord.

Revelation 4:2,3 speaks of this marvelous throne of God:

Behold, a throne set in heaven,
and One sat on the throne.
And He who sat there was like a jasper
and a sardius stone in appearance; and there
was a rainbow around the throne,
in appearance like an emerald.

Revelation chapter 4 goes on to describe all that takes place around this throne and comes out from it. What a majestic sight it is! In Revelation 5:11-14 a marvelous scene of worship, singing, and praise occurs around that throne as all creation honors the King of all kings. Solomon's throne is just a simple illustration of this, lacking in the full majesty of God's throne but reminding us of it.

The most fascinating part of Solomon's throne is its carvings or pavings. Song of Solomon 3:10 says that its interior was "paved with love by the daughters of Jerusalem." When these courtly ladies and bridal attendants thought about the character of Solomon, they responded by carving love symbols into his throne. According to what we learn from ancient customs, this throne was probably paved, lined, or carved with scenes of lovemaking. In it we see Solomon as the great lover, once again emphasizing the role of the husband in the love relationship.

WHAT THE WEDDING MEANS
TO THE BRIDEGROOM

Song of Solomon 3:11 emphasizes what this wedding celebration meant to Solomon:

Go forth, O daughters of Zion,
and see King Solomon with the crown
with which his mother crowned him
on the day of his espousals,
the day of the gladness of his heart.

All the young ladies in Israel are invited to view the bridegroom on his wedding day and ponder carefully how he is responding. The word "espousals" is used only here in the entire Old Testament. It should probably be translated "wedding," not engagement. The relationship of the "crown" to this day fits better if it is the wedding day and not the engagement ceremony.

The "crown" given to Solomon by his mother was a symbolic act of approval and blessing. Like a laurel wreath of triumph for an athlete or conqueror, it pictures a day of victory and celebration.

The Bible says that this wedding day which brought together Solomon and Abishag was "the day of the gladness of his heart." What a wonderful conclusion to this marvelous wedding procession and celebration! As Solomon wrote these words years later, how sweet to see that his marriage to Abishag was a day that brought great joy to his heart!

Solomon wrote in Ecclesiastes 9:9:

Live joyfully with the wife whom you love
all the days of your vain life which He has given you
under the sun, all your days of vanity;

for that is your portion in life, and in the
labor which you perform under the sun.

Many marriages would be different if husbands realized this principle and applied it: A wife is a great blessing and should fill your heart and life with joy. God wants our marriages to bring us much happiness.

Solomon wrote in Proverbs 5:18, "Rejoice with the wife of your youth." In Proverbs 12:4 he said, "An excellent wife is the crown of her husband." In Proverbs 18:22 he emphasized, "He who finds a wife finds a good thing, and obtains favor from the Lord."

Does the day of your marriage bring joy and gladness to your heart, or do you wish that you had never been married? Is your wife filling your mind and heart with joy, or do you wish you had married someone else?

Weddings are wonderful, but as we know so well, they are only the beginning. After the wedding comes the marrige. A good wedding helps to get a couple started right, but sometimes weddings deceive us. What we wake up with is not what we saw at the wedding! Fantasy becomes reality, and flowers turn into hair curlers and bad breath! The bride can't wear her bridal dress every day, nor can the bridegroom wear that tux to work. We can't always have the same scene and situation that we experienced on our wedding day, but the joy and excitement we felt that day can continue and even increase. It can truly get better!

HOW WOULD YOU EVALUATE
YOUR MARRIAGE?

Every now and then we need to take a deep breath and take time to evaluate our marriage. Do we still have that original joy? Are we still excited about making love together? Do thoughts of our partners cause us to be thankful and to rejoice in God's institution of marriage? If not, why not? What has gone wrong? How can we get the joy back?

Starting with Song of Solomon chapter 4, this beautiful love poem is going to give intimate details about how a husband and a wife should respond to each other if they still "live joyfully" together.

A strong feature for this love song is that of sexual desire and relationship. Since this is the Word of God, we cannot help but conclude that sexual matters play a crucial role in a good marriage. When a couple speaks disparagingly about sex within marriage, trouble is not far around the corner. When a husband shows little sexual desire for his wife (no matter what the age or physical difficulties), it is often a barometer of a struggling or dying marriage. When a wife cares nothing for sex with her husband and sees it only as a necessary evil or at best a required duty, the marriage will suffer deeply and problems will occur in other areas seemingly unrelated to sex.

Sex was invented by God for the propagation of the human race—no doubt about that. But it was also intended by God to bring pleasure to husband and wife. Unfortunately, many couples still struggle with this truth. The Song of Solomon makes it abundantly clear that God wants us to enjoy each other within the boundaries of His institution of marriage.

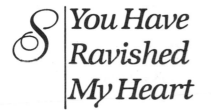

You Have Ravished My Heart

Wives, you have great ability to affect the heart of your husband. Don't ever forget that, but use it wisely and prayerfully.

The wedding night has arrived; the ceremony is over; the couple is alone. What a privilege to be spectators! Under normal conditions the bedroom is private, but God allows us to view this sexual experience for our understanding. He wants to make sure we know what to do and how to do it.

Many specific sexual techniques are missing in this love poem. You can read about them in scores of books designed to help couples adjust to each other's sexual needs and difficulties. In our opinion, the Song of Solomon is all you need. The principles and insights of sexual lovemaking presented in this book can produce a wonderful marriage relationship and bring complete sexual satisfaction. The tragedy is that so few people give it much credit. They do not explore the meaning of these romantic and poetic words or apply the kind of love which exists between Solomon and Abishag.

Two things are dealt with in the first 11 verses of chapter 4, the wedding night of Solomon and Abishag:

1. Solomon's DESCRIPTION of his wife's beauty (4:1-7).
2. Solomon's DESIRE for his wife's affection (4:8-11).

Solomon does all the talking here, suggesting that the responsibility of lovemaking rests primarily upon the husband. The wife needs reassurance that this man who dated her and spoke so romantically to her during those days is really the tender and loving husband that she expects him to be. The beginning moments of a couple's life together should be handled carefully and prayerfully. Husbands need patience, tenderness, gentleness, and loving concern for their wives, not just on the wedding night but all through the marriage.

WHAT DOES HE SEE IN HER?

Solomon's opening lines indicate what every marriage needs: a husband who is attracted to the beauty of his wife.

Behold, you are fair, my love!
Behold, you are fair!

The word "fair" means "beautiful" and is so translated by some versions of the Bible. The Israeli city of Haifa is based on this word. The root means "to shine" and has come to mean "beautiful." As visitors will attest, Haifa is a beautiful city on the Mediterranean Sea. Solomon repeats these words to emphasize how Abishag appears to him: She is beautiful.

He again calls her "my love," a word which speaks of her intimate and sexual friendship (used in 1:9,15; 2:2,10,13; 4:1,7; 5:2; and 6:4). He wants no other one but her; she is the loving friend he desires, and she is so beautiful to his eyes and heart.

Solomon describes her beauty in three ways:

1. Physically (4:1-5).
2. Emotionally (4:6).
3. Spiritually (4:7).

His physical description demonstrates how much he appreciates her loveliness, his emotional description reveals how she affects him, and his spiritual description shows how much he admires her.

SEVEN WAYS TO DESCRIBE
A WOMAN'S BODY

To those saturated with pornographic material or controlled by secular opinion, this description may seem foolish or even "nonsexy." In God's perspective, a woman's body is extremely beautiful, not because it represents a sexual object to be used or abused, but because it has been created by Him as a house for that woman's personality with all its feeling, understanding, and responses.

Separating a physical body from the person inside has serious effects upon the self-worth of that individual. When a beautiful woman is treated like a "thing" or simply a tool for a man to use in order to give him sexual satisfaction, the resulting damage to this woman's sense of dignity and self-respect is difficult to heal.

When men lack spiritual insight and emotional maturity, they often describe a woman's body in terms of their own sexual gratification. Their attention immediately centers on her breasts or sexual organs. Some husbands make a grave mistake in approaching their wives like this, thinking that this is the way to "turn them on." Solomon begins with her eyes. He reveals what a loving husband would say when he describes his wife's physical assets.

1. *He describes her eyes.*

You have dove's eyes behind your veil.

The dove was a very special bird, known for intense loyalty to its mate. Solomon sees fidelity or loyalty in Abishag's eyes. They are having a powerful effect upon him even though the wedding veil is still covering her face. This suggests that Solomon is tender in his approach rather than being quick, aggressive, and demanding. He wants to savor this moment of looking into her eyes.

When he looks at her, he experiences what she is feeling for him, and he knows in that moment that she has given herself completely to him and wants no one else.

The dove is also a symbol of purity and innocence (cf. Matthew 10:16), and it is clear to Solomon that Abishag is entering this relationship as a virgin.

Today's women often speak of the "double standard" which they believe most males have lived under for some time. It means that the man can be disloyal but the woman cannot. We certainly do not encourage such freedom for either partner, but we are also against the "double standard." Interestingly, Abishag says of Solomon in 5:12, "his eyes are like doves." A wife should be able to look deeply into her husband's eyes and see his loyalty.

Looking into each other's eyes is a very romantic thing to do, especially if you take your time. Many couples have confessed to us that they simply don't do this, or that they find it hard to do. This is not healthy. Couples should be able to look directly at each other and communicate their love for each other. The eyes are the doors into the soul, and they reveal much if we take the time to look.

2. *He describes her hair.*

Your hair is like a flock of goats
going down from Mount Gilead.

Solomon used this description again in 6:5. Some interpreters think that because goats in the Middle East have a tendency to be black, this wording is describing the color of
Abishag's hair. It may be, but there is more. "Mount Gilead"
is the key: It refers to the mountains and hills east of the Jordan
River.

When you stand on the western side of the Jordan River
and look eastward, especially at sundown, you often see herds-
men bringing their flock down from the high plateaus of
Gilead to their dwelling places in the fertile valley below.
Watching those flocks descend the hills, with the sun behind
you and reflecting off the herds, is a beautiful sight—almost
hypnotic. There is a sense of beauty as well as quiet; it is a
peaceful scene. The flowing movement of those goats and their
hair as they come down the mountain with the sun reflecting
on them is what Solomon is seeing.

If the eyes reveal his wife's *purity*, then the hair pictures
tranquility. Solomon is indeed entranced by the natural beauty
of his wife's hair. . .gentle, soft, flowing hair, inviting him
to touch its strands and lay his face within its peacefulness.
What a picture!

3. *He describes her teeth.*

Your teeth are like a flock of shorn sheep
which have come up from the washing,
every one of which bears twins,
and none is barren among them.

This flock is pictured in a unique way: right after it has
been shorn and the wool washed in water. The sheep now
appear smooth, a pinkish white in color, and glistening as the

sun bounces off their moisture. It is possible that Solomon saw his wife's teeth as glistening with the moisture of her lips and mouth. Pretty romantic, when you think about it!

The statement "every one of which bears twins" is medically correct: Your teeth come in pairs. Solomon is saying that her teeth are all evenly matched. The phrase "and none is barren among them" is also important: It means that she still has all her teeth!

The overall impression that we get from this verse is that her teeth are everything they should be in full growth and maturity. The picture of maturity emphasizes that she is ready for marriage and the experience of adult lovemaking.

4. *He describes her lips.*

> *Your lips are like a strand of scarlet,*
> *and your mouth is lovely.*

Kissing is delightful and certainly a mark of affection. But kissing in ancient times was also a mark of loyalty, and we believe that this is probably the emphasis there. One cannot help but think of the kiss of betrayal which Judas used in the Garden of Gethsemene on the cheek of Jesus. Believers are exhorted in the New Testament to give a "holy kiss" to one another, a sign of their loving relationship and loyalty to each other.

Loyalty must be on Solomon's mind as he compared Abishag's lips to a "strand [thread] of scarlet." This reminds us of Joshua 2:18 and the scarlet strand which Rahab put out of her window, indicating her loyalty to the God of Israel and His people. Cosmetics were used in Solomon's day, and we believe that her lips (especially on the wedding night) would have been made beautiful by them. But the emphasis here is not on the color of her lips but on the loyalty which the kisses of her lips would demonstrate.

Her mouth was "lovely" to him, and so should every wife's mouth be to her husband (cf. 1:5; 2:14; 6:4). A man should desire the kisses of his wife's mouth (cf. 1:2) and a wife should respond in the same way. Husbands and wives should kiss each other frequently, and a day should not go by without a warm embrace and affectionate kiss on the lips. When that becomes difficult, one can be sure there are deeper problems.

5. *He describes her temples.*

Your temples behind your veil
are like a piece of pomegranate.

Notice that the veil has not yet been removed. Solomon is taking his time.

The pomegranate has a red-and-white skin which reminded the ancient poets of modesty or the blushing of the cheeks. Some interpreters refer this to passion and excitement as well as modesty, and that is possible. The "temple" should be more properly translated "cheeks," as they simply describe the soft sides of the face. How beautiful to observe the blushing of the cheeks, and how sad when the hardness of a woman's heart can no longer reflect this quality!

Even in the physical description of his wife's body, Solomon is praising his wife's inner qualities—a good lesson for all husbands to learn!

6. *He describes her neck.*

Your neck is like the tower of David,
built for an armory, on which hang
a thousand bucklers, all shields of mighty men.

The tower of David was a special tower—a military fortress upon which the people depended for security and safety. David could be trusted to protect them, and it became a symbol of his integrity. The neck, certainly a strong point of the physical body, was often used as a symbol of strength, and in particular, strength of character.

This woman had a lot to her; she was no "pushover." She

had a mind of her own and feelings which needed to be respected and understood. She was not committing herself to be a slave to Solomon's every wish. He had many such people in his employment, but she was not going to be a doormat for him to walk on. She had integrity and strength, and Solomon admired those qualities in her.

7. *He describes her breasts.*

Your two breasts are like two fawns,
twins of a gazelle, which feed among the lilies.

No physical asset of a woman so attracts a man as the beauty of her breasts. In terms of physical anatomy, one could question why that part of a woman's body does so when there are many other parts which are beautiful in themselves, but that's the way God intended it to be.

The description "two fawns, twins of a gazelle, which feed among the lilies" has puzzled many people. What is the point here? The gazelle is like a deer, though perhaps more graceful and quick. The picture here is of two small, young, and playful animals. The height of these animals at this point in their young lives may be no more than two or three feet. They are soft to the touch and seem to display lightness and gracefulness. They are quite warm and affectionate as well as playful.

The quality which Solomon sees in the breasts of his lovely bride is that of desirability. He's saying that he longs to touch or caress them, and definitely sees the need for gentle and tender handling, not violent and aggressive behavior.

It perhaps remains a mystery as to why, but God has placed within a man's heart the natural desire to admire and fondle the breasts of a woman. God has also given a woman a certain joy and response for a man who is attracted by her breasts and knows how to gently and lovingly caress them.

Solomon makes it clear in Proverbs 5:19,20 that a husband's

desire needs to be controlled by his wife's breasts and not someone else's!

A review:

1. Eyes = purity.
2. Hair = tranquility.
3. Teeth = maturity.
4. Lips = loyalty.
5. Cheeks = modesty.
6. Neck = integrity.
7. Breasts = desirability.

HOW A WIFE AFFECTS
A MAN EMOTIONALLY

After describing the beauty of her physical body, Solomon adds a word about his emotional attraction to her.

Until the day breaks and the shadows flee away,
I will go my way to the mountain of myrrh
and to the hill of frankincense.

This is perhaps Solomon's answer to Abishag's request in 2:17 where she said:

Until the day breaks and the shadows flee away,
turn, my beloved, and be like a gazelle
or a young stag upon the mountains of Bether.

The mountains of Bether (meaning "separation") are probably symbolic for her desire to be alone with him. Now he is responding to that request. Being with her is not simply a desire to be alone, separated from everyone else (2:17), but it is like the sweetest perfume to his nostrils—an absolute delight to his heart (4:6).

Some commentators believe that the mention of two

mountains after the reference to the breasts in 4:5 implies that he is thinking of her breasts. We can't make that connection clearly. The phrase "until the day breaks and the shadows flee away" clearly picks up her words in 2:17. What we believe Solomon is doing here is reassuring her that her desire to be alone with him is also his desire, and that it is sweet to him, like the smell of myrrh and frankincense. The reference to "mountain" would also make this last connection more probable.

DO YOU ADMIRE YOUR WIFE'S FIDELITY?

Solomon adds a spiritual note to all that he has said in terms of physical and emotional attraction. In 4:7 he says:

> *You are all fair, my love,*
> *and there is no spot in you.*

He reminds her again of how beautiful she is to his heart and eyes, but he especially emphasizes her purity: "no spot in you." These words are used of sacrificial animals that are acceptable for worship. He is greatly attracted by her purity.

In this day of easy sex and numerous encounters, it's time to take a second look at the subject of remaining a virgin until marriage. The Bible teaches it, and the continuing problems of illicit sexual relationships also argue for it. Do you want the greatest amount of happiness all the days of your life? Then remain a virgin until you are married. You will be so glad you did in the years ahead!

THE HUSBAND'S DESIRE FOR LOVE

Four times in these verses Solomon calls Abishag "my spouse" or "my bride." The wedding has taken place, and he is so thrilled to say to her, "You are my wife; you belong to me!"

Solomon indicates that a husband's desire for the love of his wife involves four things:

1. Being alone with her (4:8).
2. Being aroused by her (4:9).
3. Being attracted by her lovemaking (4:10).
4. Being affected by her sweetness and smell (4:11).

BEING ALONE

Sometimes being alone is not easy to do! Some couples try to avoid being alone together because their relationship is not what it should be. A healthy marriage will always find the husband desiring to be alone with his wife.

Come with me from Lebanon, my spouse,
with me from Lebanon. Look from the top of Amana,
from the top of Senir and Hermon, from the
lions' dens, from the mountains of the leopards.

We struggled with this passage quite a bit. The longer we tried to find specific significance to each phrase and word, the more we seemed to miss the major point. Solomon wants to be alone with his bride, and he describes places and situations which would touch the heart of a country girl who loves the out-of-doors. He is in the bedchamber of the palace on their wedding night, but he is also drawing her heart after him as he pictures faraway places and secluded spots. It is romance from beginning to end, and she does not miss the point or fail to feel his strong desire for her!

One young couple who found their marriage somewhat less than what they expected talked to us about their sex life.

It had become boring, dull, routine, and unfulfilling even though they had been married only two years. We suggested two days in a motel away from their surroundings. Today (many years later) they still speak about the practical advice we gave. We didn't think it was all that earthshaking, but they said it did wonders for them.

We have also discussed this matter with couples who have been married for many years. There is a great need to be alone, completely away from your present circumstances and surroundings, so that the two of you can concentrate on your relationship and can make love to each other without interruptions.

BEING AROUSED

You have ravished my heart, my sister, my spouse;
you have ravished my heart
with one look of your eyes,
with one link of your necklace.

The New International Version of the Bible says "You have stolen my heart." The New American Standard Bible says "You have made my heart beat faster." The man is getting aroused! Her eyes (like a dove) are continuing to affect him. It appears as though the veil has now been removed and that he is looking directly into those beautiful eyes of Abishag. He can hardly contain himself.

The necklace she is wearing on her wedding night seems to capture her beauty in a special way, and he is attracted by it. There are times when we need to dress up for each other. Refusing to be attractive has no merit, even when we proclaim the glory of "being natural." The Song of Solomon is not against cosmetics or jewelry, although the New Testament warns of public display and extravagant use of these things.

BEING ATTRACTED

When a wife asks us whether she should be aggressive in lovemaking, we wonder if she has read the Song of Solomon carefully. Solomon refers to her sexual responses to him in 4:10:

How fair is your love, my sister, my spouse!
How much better than wine is your love,
and the scent of your perfumes than all spices!

The word "love" in this verse refers to lovemaking. In 1:2 Abishag said about Solomon, "Your love is better than wine." Now he says the same about her.

Solomon describes how beautiful is her lovemaking, better than any earthly celebration ("wine"). The very smell of her is better than all the fragrances in the world. The moistness of her feminine passion is attracting him. She is responding to his tenderness and gracious words about her beauty, for a woman responds greatly to loving and kind words. He is now being attracted greatly by her responses to him, and every husband knows that such response is irresistible!

BEING AFFECTED

Your lips, O my spouse, drip as the honeycomb;
honey and milk are under your tongue;
and the fragrance of your garments is like
the fragrance of Lebanon.

This is really getting romantic! The reference to her lips and tongue and how they are affecting him suggests that they have begun to caress each other and that her kisses and sexual responses are having their intended effect on him.

Wives, you have great ability to affect the heart of your husband. Don't ever forget that, but use it wisely and prayerfully. If you want to motivate him, don't be critical or withdraw from him. We understand that it is difficult for you to respond to a man who does not love you like Solomon, but don't suppress your God-given ability to affect him. Your sexual responses to him are vital to your relationship and his attitudes toward you. We don't want to put a burden on you that is unrealistic or unjustified, for he needs to respond to God's love as well, but we want you to see what kind of impact you can have on your husband if you really use what God has given you.

Come to My Garden
(Adults Only)

SONG OF SOLOMON • 4:12–5:1

*When two people love each other intensely and
have committed their lives and marriage to the
Lord Himself, relying upon His Holy Spirit to fill
them and use them, there is no limit to the
sexual pleasure and enjoyment they can experience.*

Solomon has expressed his love verbally, and now he
will express it physically. This is the climax of their
desire for each other, the celebration of their wedding
night!

Sexual pleasure should be experienced in marriage!

One of the greatest misunderstandings that some couples
have about marriage is that sex was not intended for pleasure.
This has sometimes resulted from teachings that certain
churches have forwarded in order to combat secular views.

Sex was invented by God. Its purpose included human
reproduction and sexual satisfaction in order to avoid sexual
immorality (Genesis 1:26-28; 1 Corinthians 7:1-5). The Song
of Solomon clearly presents a picture of sexual passion, arousal,

and intimate pleasure. We should not allow worldly view-points to corrupt this sacred blessing from God. The Bible gives no authorization to sexual pleasure outside of marriage—that is quite clear. But *within* marriage sex is God's blessing for husband and wife. It was meant to be enjoyed.

This beautiful passage of sexual pleasure is based upon four important principles, each critically important if the sexual relationship of husband and wife is to be all that God originally intended.

PLEASURE PRINCIPLE NUMBER ONE

Sexual pleasure is based on the attraction of the husband to his wife.

Solomon pictures the sexual delights of his wife, Abishag, as though she were a "garden." Similar word pictures are found in the writings of ancient cultures in love poetry. Plants, fruits, fragrances, etc. were all used as erotic symbols, picturing the sexual relationship and pleasures of marriage.

Sexual pleasure is most difficult when the husband is not attracted to the wife. When the husband simply uses her to satisfy his sexual needs and treats her as a sexual object, the wife will usually not experience any pleasure in the relationship.

Solomon was attracted by several things, all of which deepened the passion and love relationship which they shared as a couple. He was delighted with his wife and did not hesitate to describe her sexuality in beautiful and romantic terms.

He was attracted by her fidelity.

A garden enclosed is my sister, my spouse,
a spring shut up, a fountain sealed.

The emphasis here is on the fact that she is a virgin. She has protected her sexual fruits and delicious waters from others and saved them for the one she would marry. Solomon is deeply attracted to this commitment.

Abishag's sexuality is described as a "garden," a "spring," and a "fountain." Solomon found her "enclosed," "shut up," and "sealed." Obviously from 4:16, Abishag has now removed the locks and barriers and invited Solomon to enjoy himself.

Solomon uses similar language in Proverbs 5:15-20 in warning us about premarital or extramarital sex:

Drink water from your own cistern, and running water from your own well. Should your fountains be dispersed abroad, streams of water in the streets? Let them be only your own, and not for strangers with you. Let your fountain be blessed, and rejoice with the wife of your youth. As a loving deer and a graceful doe, let her breasts satisfy you at all times; and always be enraptured with her love. For why should you, my son, be enraptured by an immoral woman, and be embraced in the arms of a seductress?

Sound advice! The picture is the same as in the Song of Solomon, and the importance of virginity before marriage is emphasized in no uncertain terms. The "garden" should remain off-limits to any person besides your marital partner. Your "fountain" will be blessed by God with sexual vitality and pleasure when its "streams" flow only toward your spouse.

The young man in David's office was deeply disturbed. He was engaged to be married but had just found out that his bride-to-be was not a virgin and had in fact had sexual relationships with another young man during the days of their courtship. He was heartbroken, and wondered if he should go through with the marriage. God's forgiveness is a wonderful thing, but this engagement had been broken by sexual immorality and this young man was suffering because of it.

He tried to forgive his girlfriend, but it became too much

for him to handle and the marriage was called off. No matter what we might think about what he did, it is a reminder to all of us of the emotional damage which infidelity causes, even during the engagement period. God honors those who stay away from sexual sin, and even promises great sexual pleasure and satisfaction in marriage to those who abide by His standards. This is a hard lesson to learn. We are often pressured to ignore God's advice or tempted to think that we will experience no consequences of our actions. How foolish we are!

He was attracted by her fruits.

*Your plants are an orchard
of pomegranates with pleasant fruits.*

The word "plants" is referring to her sexuality. Solomon saw her as an "orchard of pomegranates" and not just as one tree or one plant. There were many facets to her sexual desires and delights. Her "fruits" were "pleasant," a delight to his heart. These symbols of love are all intended to emphasize the pleasure which can be experienced within the marriage relationship.

The word "fruits" indicated the joy of tasting and eating. The erotic overtones of this romantic passage are quite obvious, and commentators who try to avoid it or allegorize these words are missing the point. A worse consequence is when allegorical interpretations lead us to believe that sexual pleasure is not the intention of God for marriage.

He was attracted by her fragrances.

*Fragrant henna with spikenard,
spikenard and saffron, calamus and cinnamon,
with all trees of frankincense, myrrh and aloes,
with all the chief spices.*

It is possible that these smells were the result of Abishag being bathed in exotic perfumes, which were readily available and were collected by King Solomon from all over the world. Certainly the wedding night would be one of those occasions when such fragrances would be abundantly used.

However, the point of this passage is that Abishag herself causes these smells. These are her "plants" and her "spices." Solomon is speaking of her sexuality and how wonderful is her smell in the midst of lovemaking. How sweet of Solomon to speak of this to his bride and to assure her that he continued to be attracted by all that she brings forth!
He was attracted by her fountain.

*A fountain of gardens, a well of
living waters, and streams from Lebanon.*

What beautiful and romantic language! Her sexual response to him was like "living waters" and the delicious-tasting "streams of Lebanon" that come down the slopes of Mount Hermon. How wonderfully refreshing they are! Solomon pictures his bride that way. Her sexuality is like the most delicious-tasting water—nothing can compare with it.

It is possible (though not conclusive) that Solomon is referring to the sexual release of his bride in these beautiful phrases. If so, then we must say that no book written by human ingenuity could possibly improve on or add anything more to our sexual understanding. This is God's Word, and though our human interpretation is fallible and often misses the mark of what God intended, we believe that everything written in this beautiful Song of Songs is infallible and the very best instruction that any married couple could possibly obtain.

In one of our marriage seminars during a question-and-answer session, a wife asked this question on a piece of paper without giving her name: "Is a wife supposed to have a sexual release?" She went on to describe the frustration she had experienced in her relationship with her husband. She said that he was so quick in his sexual lovemaking that she never had enough time to feel anything. She explained on a rather lengthy note that she felt selfish in her desires, and wondered if the Bible had anything to say about this. Maybe, she concluded, it was not the will of God for the wife to experience sexual pleasure. Perhaps the wife's role was simply to please her husband.

Similar questions (though embarrassing to deal with) are asked by other wives who are confused or disappointed in sexual relationships with their husbands. If we understand the Song of Solomon correctly, wives as well as husbands are to experience sexual pleasure. This means that husbands need to be sensitive and loving in their understanding and approach to their wives and their sexual needs. First Corinthians 7:3 commands:

> *Let the husband render to his wife*
> *the affection due her, and likewise also*
> *the wife to her husband.*

The Bible teaches a mutual responsibility. Sexual pleasure and satisfaction should never be one-sided.

After Solomon describes his wife's sexuality and its great attractiveness to him, she brings forth a romantic and passionate invitation for him to enjoy what he sees and feels from her love for him. Though poetic, these words are clear evidence of the Bible's emphasis on sexual pleasure within a marriage. They are spoken by the wife to her husband. All inhibitions and reluctance to engage in sexual pleasure are now set side. She is ready to receive his sexual desire.

PLEASURE PRINCIPLE NUMBER TWO

Sexual pleasure is based on the attitude of the wife toward her husband's desire.

A Christian wife was struggling with the sexual desires and passion she saw in her husband. He was a good man and loved the Lord, but he was hurting from her reluctance. We tried to talk to them about God's love, but we sensed that there was more to her story than we were hearing.

Carole was able to identify with her, and helped her to relax and share what was bothering her. It seems that her mother had planted the thought in her head that men were animals, and that their sexual desires were nothing but carnal passion, unrelated to true spiritual love. It was something to be endured, not enjoyed. Men were to be pitied for "their problem." She seemed surprised when Carole shared the Bible's view of sexual desire and pleasure.

After several occasions in which these issues were discussed with a Christian female counselor, this wife began to see her problem. She was able to confess to her husband and ask for his forgiveness. She literally set him free, and their marriage started to grow once more. The interesting thing was how much his public ministry changed. He had a new joy and freedom in sharing God's Word with other people, and definitely seemed more relaxed and contented.

> *Awake, O north wind, and come, O south!*
> *Blow upon my garden, that its spices*
> *may flow out. Let my beloved come to his*
> *garden and eat its pleasant fruits.*

In Song of Solomon 2:7 and 3:5 she had previously said, "Do not awaken love." Now she says, "Awake!" The prohibition was necessary before marriage; after the wedding no such restriction is applied.

Three things are obvious from this beautiful and romantic verse, spoken at the height of their sexual love and passion for each other:

1. *She desires him greatly:* "awake...and come."

She states, "Let my beloved come to his garden." She wants him, and in a sense has let her passion and desire run uncontrolled. After all, she is in the safety and security of his love and protection. Her marriage vows have insured the validity and morality of this moment. No restraint is necessary.

2. *She wants to give her sexuality to him:* "that its spices may flow out."

He has described her sexuality with the same words, and she picks up on his sensuous remarks and gives approval and agreement to them. She wants to let go and give to him completely. In the security and commitment of marriage, there is nothing sweeter or more satisfying than giving yourself and all that you feel to the person you love and the one to whom you are committed. What joy can fill our hearts at that moment! God has been so gracious to allow us this sacred priviledge within marriage. What a blessing from His loving hand!

3. *She wants him to enjoy himself:* "eat its pleasant fruits."

She is not resisting this moment. She has no condemnation of his sexual passion and desires. She rejoices in them and wants him to experience everything possible from her "fruits." There is not a husband on earth who would refuse such an invitation if it were bathed in God's love and a deeply committed marital relationship. Sinful practices and attitudes can severely damage such a moment, of course. But God's standard of sexual happiness is clearly presented here in this beautiful love song.

When two people love each other intensely and have committed their lives and marriage to the Lord Himself, relying upon His Holy Spirit to fill them and use them, there is no limit to the sexual pleasure and enjoyment they can experience.

PLEASURE PRINCIPLE NUMBER THREE

Sexual pleasure is based on the acceptance of sexual satisfaction and unity by both husband and wife.

I have come to my garden, my sister, my spouse;
I have gathered my myrrh with my spice;
I have eaten my honeycomb with my honey;
I have drunk my wine with my milk.

Both partners must agree with what takes place when they make love with each other. Sexual pleasure depends on such mutual acceptance by both partners. When one partner disagrees with what is desired or practiced, it will be difficult for sexual pleasure to be experienced and enjoyed as it should be.

Notice how this verse blends things together:

"my myrrh with my spice"
"my honeycomb with my honey"
"my wine with my milk"

These combinations reveal that both partners are enjoying their sexual relationship and are finding it as satisfying as they had desired when they started. That's the way it should be in any marriage ruled by God's Word and controlled by His love.

Often we are asked about the morality and validity of certain sexual acts and practices within marriage. From a technical side, everything within marriage is acceptable, while anything outside of marriage is denied.

But more needs to be said. When one partner demands a certain sexual activity from the other partner, it is unlikely that it will produce sexual pleasure or happiness. Usually one partner suffers.

It is true that the Bible teaches mutual submission in the marriage relationship (1 Corinthians 7:1-5). However, insisting on your rights often alienates the one you supposedly love and damages the emotional and spiritual unity you should also be enjoying. We believe it is better to ask the following questions:

1. Is there anything I am currently doing that is offensive to you or you would rather not do?
2. Is there something you would like to do that we are not currently doing?

Asking these questions can help, but be sure you are ready to respond affirmatively to your partner. If your partner answers yes to question number one, are you willing to refrain from that practice until your partner has peace about it? Are you patient and loving enough to discuss it and to share the reasons why you want to do it and feel it would enhance your sexual relationship as a married couple?

If your partner answers question number two by telling you about a certain practice that may not seem enjoyable to you, would you be willing to do it for the benefit and enjoyment of your partner? Could you put your heart into it, knowing that it was a blessing to your partner though not to you?

These are important questions. We believe that sexual pleasure is very much related to sexual understanding and unity. Marital partners should be in agreement about what takes place in the bedroom.

PLEASURE PRINCIPLE NUMBER FOUR

Sexual pleasure is based on the approval of God.

Eat, O friends! Drink, yes, drink deeply,
O beloved ones!

Who is speaking in this verse? Some say that these words are spoken by the daughters of Jerusalem, who are observing the married couple on their wedding night! This we find hard to accept, because it is none of their business what Solomon and Abishag do in terms of their sexual pleasure. That's why we don't share in this book what we actually do together as a married couple. We all have the Song of Solomon to read, and this book says it all as far as we are concerned. What more could be added to the romantic love that is pictured in this marvelous book?

Here are some of the viewpoints about these words in Song of Solomon 5:1b:

1. Spoken by the wedding guests.
2. Spoken by the daughters of Jerusalem.
3. Spoken by angels.

Some people suggest that Luke 15:7,10 speaks of the joy of angels in heaven over one sinner that repents. Perhaps they also observe what humans experience sexually and rejoice with us on that matter as well. Without more evidence, we find this view hard to accept.

4. Spoken by God Himself.

We think the best view is that God is doing the speaking. If this is so, then sexual pleasure has the direct approval of God Himself.

Hebrews 13:4 seems to agree with this when it states:

Marriage is honorable among all,
and the bed undefiled; but fornicators
and adulterers God will judge.

The word "bed" (Greek *coitus*) implies that sex within marriage is not defiling or sinful.

If God is speaking in Song of Solomon 5:1b, then He invited this couple to "drink deeply." This means to be intoxicated with each other's sexual desire and passion. It matches the teaching of Proverbs 5:18-20, where the same idea of intoxication is used.

When sexual pleasure is enjoyed to its fullest, the feeling

is like being intoxicated. Your mind, emotions, and responses are carried away by the drawing power of sexual passion and desire.

In marriage, a couple is simply giving to each other, and the result is edification, building each other up and strengthening each other's life. When it takes place outside of marriage, the sexual vitality is lost. In marriage it is replaced and held by the other partner.

What a beautiful relationship has been pictured in these verses! Husband and wife, mutually giving to each other their respective desires and passion: no restraint...no reluctance... no inhibitions...no fears...no selfishness. Here is romantic love from God's point of view!

10 | Not Tonight!

SONG OF SOLOMON • 5:2-8

---

*The Bible does not try to hide the fact
of human weakness and selfishness.
As most married couples know quite well,
all is not perfect in the bedroom!*

---

*I*n the previous chapter we were allowed to see the beautiful lovemaking of Solomon and Abishag and to understand the principle that sexual pleasure should be experienced in marriage. It was a beautiful relationship to observe, and was given the approval of God Himself.

The Bible does not try to hide the fact of human weakness and selfishness. As most married couples know quite well, all is not perfect in the bedroom! There are problems at times that strain our relationships and cause us to withdraw from the delights of sexual love.

Abishag has another dream that focuses on a common problem within the sexual relationship of husband and wife. Jokes are frequently given regarding this problem, but it really is not funny, especially if you are experiencing it at the present time. The problem starts when one partner does not feel like responding sexually to the other. No matter what the reason, it usually becomes something more than the partner anticipated. Hurt feelings easily develop, and anger often results.

One middle-aged man asked in a question-and-answer session about sex, "Why do women have so many headaches? Right about the time I am in the mood for love, my wife seems to get a terrible headache and is unable to make love because of it!" He was frustrated and a little hostile about it.

One young wife told us that she was not going to make love with her husband until he started helping her around the house. Her words were, "Who does he think he is?"

A wife with three children told us, "My husband thinks that I can just jump into bed with him at a moment's notice! Does he really know how exhausting it is to handle three small children all day?"

It goes both ways. A husband noted that his wife is expecting too much sex from him and he frankly doesn't have the desire or energy that she does.

A wife in her fifties told us, "My husband always finds something else to do. I really enjoy making love with him, but he seems to feel that once a month is enough!"

The stories repeat themselves no matter what the age of the couples involved. When you refuse to meet the sexual needs of your partner, no matter how justified you may feel in that reluctance, your partner is hurt. Sometimes it is not evident right away, but in a few days or weeks you begin to notice a touch of resentment and tension.

JUST A DREAM?

Abishag says in Song of Solomon 5:2:

I sleep, but my heart is awake.

She is having a dream. The dream extends at least through 5:8, and contains a vital message for all couples. The point of the dream is that sexual problems in marriage must be resolved. Don't expect them to go away by themselves. In time they have a way of rising up to afflict your love relationship with each other. A barrier to your communication with each other can often be caused by the simple neglect of your partner's sexual desires and needs.

BAD TIMING

In her dream, Abishag pictures her husband coming home late from work and desiring to make love with her after she has already gone to bed. Verse 2 reveals his desire for her and the approximate time in which this occurred.

It is the voice of my beloved! He knocks,
saying, "Open for me, my sister, my love,
my dove, my perfect one; for my head is covered
with dew, my locks with the drops of the night."

She recognizes his voice and identified him as "my beloved." Her heart always responded to the sweetness of his voice and the encouragement which he brought to her heart, but for some reason she did not respond. It must have been shocking to her to have dreamed this in the light of their love for each other, but it does happen. We are only human, and quite prone to selfishness.

His loving appeal emphasized the glory of their relationship to each other. He called her "my sister, my love, my dove, my perfect one." What more could she ask? He loved everything about her and could hardly wait to be with her once more.

The clue to the bad timing is his statement "My head is covered with dew, my locks with the drops of the night." This suggests the early hours of the morning. Perhaps some serious political strategy meeting has kept him up this night, or some economic problems have troubled his kingdom. We don't know what happened; we just know that he has come home very late.

Husbands should be careful about coming home late and not informing their wives about it. There was no telephone in Solomon's day, but we have them today. They can be a curse, but they are also a blessing. A simple call to explain why you are going to be late is most helpful. Husbands who make a frequent practice of coming home late are hurting their wives. The damage may be hard to repair, and the suspicions and jealousies can develop rapidly. Why are you so late all the time? Is there someone else in your life?

SELFISH REASONS

*I have taken off my robe;
how can I put it on again? I have washed my feet;
how can I defile them?*

To people today, this sounds a little strange. First of all, why does she have to get up? If she is in bed, why doesn't Solomon just jump in with her? Secondly, why would her feet get dirty if she made love with him? What does washing her feet have to do with making love?

In ancient times, special bridal chambers were prepared for the wives of kings. It was like her own apartment or bedroom. The palace had many rooms and scores of people living there. A special bedroom was designed for the wife of the king, and it was there that he would make love with her. The door to this bedroom or bridal chamber had a lock system with a board or rod across the door on the inside to prevent anyone from getting into the room. To open the door, one would have to lift up that board. Usually there was an opening in the door through which one could slip his hand and lift the board up, provided that it was not locked in place by a person on the inside.

Solomon approaches the door and realizes that Abishag has it locked from the inside. He speaks words of love to her and urges her to open the door so that he can come in and spend this night with her. She is evidently so tired that she can't seem to be motivated enough to get up, put her robe on, and walk across the room to open the door. Besides, she would get her feet dirty again, and she had had one of those wonderful Oriental baths early that evening.

It may not seem like much of an excuse, and in one sense it wasn't. But many married couples today withhold sex from each other for more trivial reasons.

The good news is that Abishag still loves him very much, even in her dream. She says in 5:4:

My beloved put his hand by the latch of the door,
and my heart yearned for him.

She realizes that he is reaching his hand through the opening and trying to lift the board that is barring the door. But it is locked. Knowing how much she loves him and he loves her, she senses in her dream that she should get up and let him in. But she responds too late. Verses 5 and 6 say:

I arose to open for my beloved,
and my hands dripped with myrrh,
my fingers with liquid myrrh, on the handles
of the lock. I opened for my beloved,
but my beloved had turned away and was gone.
My heart went out to him when he spoke.
I sought him, but I could not find him;
I called him, but he gave me no answer.

It was a custom in ancient times to leave a message in the opening of the door if it was locked and no one came to open the door. One such custom was for a lover to leave some sweet-smelling ointment or perfume on the handles of the lock. It was his way of saying that he still loved her very much.

Abishag was heartbroken when she finally responded. It was too late—he was gone. Her heart went with him, and she began an intense search to find him. She called out to him, but there was no answer.

WHAT IS THE POINT?

The message is quite clear if you will simply take a moment to reflect on it. It is never right to withhold sex from your marital partner. You not only hurt your partner but you also hurt yourself.

The New Testament teaches the same principle. First Corinthians 7:5 says:

> *Do not deprive one another except with consent*
> *for a time, that you may give yourselves*
> *to fasting and prayer; and come together again*
> *so that Satan does not tempt you*
> *because of your lack of self-control.*

The word "consent" in Greek demands mutual agreement. It is never right to withhold sex from your partner unless you both agree to it. There is also a serious warning in this verse about staying away from sex for too long a time. Satan knows our sexual needs and weaknesses, and he will tempt us greatly because he knows we are vulnerable in this area. The verse says that we do not have self-control.

Some Christians think that this verse does not apply to them. They assume that this would never be their problem and that they do have control over their sexual appetites. How foolish we can be!

We remember well a young man who told us that God was leading him to work overseas for several months and that his wife would not be going with him. She was not happy with his decision and was quite concerned about what might happen to their relationship. But he rebuked her for not trusting him and felt that we were guilty of the same thing. We pointed out the danger to him, but he seemed to think that it was not a problem for him. He told us that he had gone a few weeks without sex before and did not feel pressured. He was sure he could handle it.

We were disturbed that he and his wife did not agree on his decision, and we were also concerned about the length of time involved. Eight months after he was gone, we received word that he was now involved with a woman overseas and wanted a divorce from his wife. What a tragedy!

SENSING GUILT

In her dream, Abishag searches for Solomon throughout the city but cannot find him. She encounters the guards, but because she is not wearing her royal attire, they treat her without respect.

> *The watchmen who went about the city*
> *found me. They struck me, they wounded me;*
> *the keepers of the walls took*
> *my veil away from me.*

She dreams that her right to be Solomon's bride is removed. Because she refused to make love with Solomon, she suffers physical abuse, being treated as a woman of the streets, and suffers the emotional trauma of losing her position as Solomon's bride. What a dream!

Imagine waking up after a dream like that! No wonder she starts describing Solomon the way she does in the latter part of chapter 5! She wants everyone to know how much she loves him. Her dream taught her a powerful lesson that all married couples should apply:

> Regardless of how you feel, always respond immediately to your spouse's sexual desires.

WHAT ABISHAG LEARNED

Abishag responds to what she dreamed by giving this charge to the daughters of Jerusalem in 5:8:

> *I charge you, O daughters of Jerusalem,*
> *if you find my beloved, that you tell him I am lovesick!*

She wants Solomon to know that she is sorry for refusing him that night and that she is filled with passion and desire for his lovemaking. She is saying by this response that she will always be ready for his love and available to meet his needs. She indicates by what she says that it will not be a matter of duty or obligation that will motivate her, but love for him. It will not be a passive partner that he will encounter, but one who is ready and filled with passion, responsive to his love and desiring his lovemaking.

Any husband would be thrilled to know that his wife feels this way about him. Carole and I have discussed these matters on many occasions during the years of our marriage, and we are aware of the problems that can arise. There are times when we are tired and seemingly unable to make love with each other. But we recognize the principle that if one partner needs it, the other is to respond willingly and enthusiastically. We have observed that God always honors our obedience to Him. If He commanded us to give sexually to each other no matter how we may personally feel at the time, then we should do it. The good news is that He always seems to provide us with the energy we need when we are committed to obeying His instruction, and rewards us with special feelings of love, joy, and contentment because we have obeyed Him even when we didn't feel like it.

Often we have talked about passive or disinterested sex. It is rarely rewarding to a spouse to have the other partner do it just to be doing it. When the other partner does not respond with sexual excitement or personal passion, there is a sense of loss and even of rejection.

How necessary it is for us to rely upon the power of the Holy Spirit, and how much we need God's love controlling our hearts!

11 | Altogether Lovely

Solomon was attractive to Abishag in many ways. Sweet communication and intimate friendship dominated her thoughts of him. No wonder she spoke of him as "altogether lovely"!

Physical and sensual descriptions of the male in the love poetry of the ancient world are seldom found. But in the Song of Solomon, Abishag describes her lover in beautiful and encouraging words, words that would touch the heart of any husband.

In God's kind of marriage, both husband and wife are involved. Each contributes to the other, and they work together as a team. Both know how to make love as well as communicate and build each other up.

One of the pastors on the staff of a former church related how he challenged a wife who found it hard to love her husband. He asked her to describe his positive qualities and to find things about him that she liked. Her reluctance to do so, combined with the difficulty she experienced in coming up with at least one good quality, opened up the way to some effective counseling and constructive changes in her marriage. She realized in that embarrassing moment how much she concentrated on the negative rather than the positive aspects of her husband.

A CHALLENGING QUESTION

*What is your beloved more than another
beloved, O fairest among women?
What is your beloved more than another
beloved, that you so charge us?*

These daughters of Jerusalem, the ladies of the court, are challenging Abishag about the charge she gave to them in 5:8. She wanted them to help her find her beloved and tell him how much she desired him. She said that she was lovesick.

These ladies answer with a question: "What makes him so special?" They wanted to know why she felt so strongly about him and desired their help in searching for him.

This is a good question for every wife: "Why is your husband better for you than someone else?" Of course, it's a dangerous question, especially if you have already decided that someone else would be better!

There are really two effects that this question has upon Abishag. It's a searching question demanding a thoughtful answer. Notice its effect upon Abishag.

1. *It causes her to reflect on her own beauty.*

The phrase "O fairest among women" could be taken as a sarcastic remark by these ladies, referring back to what Solomon said about her in 1:8. The point would be, "If you are so beautiful among all the women of the world, why would you need our help in finding Solomon? Would he not come to your side if you are really the best?"

Some women are so enamored with their own beauty and appearance that they fail to see the need of their husbands for love and encouragement. The most beautiful woman in the world can become quite unappealing to a man if she is more concerned about herself than other people.

We knew a woman like this many years ago. She was a beauty to behold—attractive figure, gorgeous face, lovely hair. But she was self-centered. The result was loneliness, a bad self-image, and constant feelings of rejection by others. She was more concerned about her own beauty and appearance than the needs of others around her, and so they had no desire to be friends with her. They admired her from a distance, but did not enjoy being around her.

2. *It causes her to reflect on her desires for him.*

The last phrase of their question says "that you so charge us." This takes us back to 5:8, where she charges them to help her find Solomon in order to tell him how strong her desires for him really are.

It has been often said, "Beauty is in the eye of the beholder." There's a lot of truth in that statement when it comes to marriage. When your desires for your spouse are strong, it doesn't matter what others may think—your spouse is special and better than anyone else! By their question, these ladies are challenging Abishag to think about her desires for Solomon and what that involves.

A CONFIRMING ANSWER

Abishag is not afraid of the question "What makes him so special?" She begins her answer, and will continue in chapter 6.

She describes him as the best.

My beloved is white and ruddy, chief among ten thousand. His head is like the finest gold.

The word "white" is translated by the New International Version as "radiant." The New American Standard Bible says "dazzling." We might say that he is "stunning."

The word "ruddy," which is used 21 times as an adverb and an adjective, is possibly a variation of the word for "man." The idea would be that he is manly. This "stunning" and "manly" person is also "chief among ten thousand." He is outstanding among thousands of others.

When she describes his head as the "finest gold," she is saying that he is made of the very best material. No one compares with him—he is number one in her heart!

Wives, how do you feel about your husband? Is he number one to you? Does he have first place in your heart in comparison with all other men?

We listened to a wife in our living room berate her husband (he was also there!). In her eyes he could do nothing right. He was not what he should be, and in her view he could never be what she wanted him to be. It was indeed sad to listen to her, for she did not seem to be aware of what she was doing to her husband.

A few months later we learned of an affair he had with a woman less attractive than his wife and far less talented. He was heartbroken about it, but said these interesting words: "I finally found someone who thinks I'm special!"

She depends upon his loving care and loyalty.

His locks are wavy, and black as a raven.
His eyes are like doves by the rivers
of waters, washed with milk, and fitly set.

Abishag describes two things about his character that make him so special to her heart.

1. *His hair reminds her of his loving care.*

Just as his hair adorned and covered his head, she saw how his love covered her insecurities, fears, and needs. The key here is the word "raven." In 1 Kings 17:2-6 God used ravens to bring food to Elijah to take care of his physical need. These birds are known for taking care of their own and are used in the Bible to remind us of God's loving care and protection.

2. His eyes remind her of his loyalty.

In 4:1 Solomon said that Abishag had "dove's eyes." Now she says, "His eyes are like doves." The dove is loyal to its mate all its life. As an acceptable bird for Old Testament sacrifice, the dove pictures purity.

No quality in a husband's life is so crucial to his wife's response as that of his loyalty to her. His wedding vows went something like this:

> I PLEDGE MY LOYALTY TO YOU
> AND TO YOU ALONE, UNTIL THE LORD COMES
> OR DEATH PARTS US.

No doubt you said something similar in your own marriage vows. Have you kept your word? We experience many temptations throughout our lives that lead us to consider violating our vows. But when we do, we undermine the response of our wives to our leadership and love. We need the eyes of a dove as surely as our wives do.

Don said those words of loyalty on his wedding day, and he meant them. His wife was beautiful and very supportive. One day at his office came a temptation. A girl with whom he had worked on several projects invited him to have dinner with her at her house, where they were going to work on a particular task that was assigned to them by their boss. Don should have known that this was a dangerous situation, especially when he found himself hiding the truth from his wife. He told her he had to work late on this project, but left out the details about the dinner and the girl. His eyes were something less than a dove's eyes!

To hear him tell the story months later you would think that he was totally innocent when he went to dinner that evening at this girl's house. But his excitement betrayed him. This was no simple business deal—he was sexually excited in his heart about what might develop, even though at the time he would have denied it.

You can guess what happened. And it continued. His affair came to an abrupt halt one day when the girl decided to take up with someone else. After all, she was single, and Don was married. She even said to him that she could not trust him. If he would cheat on his wife, he might cheat on her too!

Don was able to get back with his wife, and she was most gracious, loving, and forgiving, though deeply hurt. He lost his dove's eyes, and it cost him a great deal of happiness.

She desires his love and affection.

Abishag described first how Solomon was the very best, above all others. She then expressed how she depended upon his loving care and loyalty. Now she reveals how she desires his love and affection.

> *His cheeks are like a bed of spices,*
> *like banks of scented herbs. His lips are lilies,*
> *dripping liquid myrrh.*

By describing his cheeks, she simply states how she likes the way he smells. As a "bed of spices" there is a lot for her to enjoy. His cheeks smell wonderful, and picture sweetness in terms of the spices.

She also likes the way he tastes. She refers to his lips as "lilies, dripping liquid myrrh." Earlier, in 1:2, she spoke these words about his lips:

> *Let him kiss me with the kisses of his mouth—*
> *for your love is better than wine.*

She delights in his kisses. It was the same "liquid myrrh" that Solomon put on the handles of the lock in 5:5. She wants everyone to know how delightfully sweet, fragrant, and romantic are his kisses. It is another way of saying how much she desires him.

Carole and I enjoy kissing. We do so after having a prayer before we eat. It's a habit, and a great one. When I go to work in the morning, we hug and kiss. When I come home at night, we do it again. We frequently show such affection through-out the evening, long before we climb into bed with each other. We believe in loads of affection—lots of hugs and kisses. When couples are not affectionate with each other, it makes us a little apprehensive about what may be going on in their lives at home.

She delights in his strength and appearance.

His hands are rods of gold set with beryl.
His body is carved ivory inlaid with sapphires.
His legs are pillars of marble set on bases
of fine gold. His countenance is like Lebanon,
excellent as the cedars.

Let's face it, men, this man is Mr. America! How are we going to measure up to that? Let's take it slowly and see if we can find exactly what Abishag is saying about Solomon. What does she want us to know about him that makes him so attractive? Is it just a beautiful body?

1. *She delights in his hands.*

Most women love the hands of a man, for they speak of the strength of his character. Women like these hands to be gentle. How fascinating that Abishag saw Solomon's hands as "rods of gold set with beryl." Gold is a soft metal, and very pliable. It is also strong and speaks of value. The word "rods" comes from the root meaning "circle," and probably refers to the fingers. The phrase "set with beryl" might refer to the fingernails. The emphasis is on the beauty of his hands.

Most wives enjoy the caresses of their husband's hands, and the gentle touch of their fingers—strength combined with gentleness and beauty. The hands are symbols of work as well as love. Everything a man touches is affected by who he really is inside. A woman loves his sensitivity to her.

2. *She delights in his body.*

"Carved ivory" is not simply describing a strong and fat-free torso! It possibly also refers to the smoothness of his skin. She loves to touch his body and feel the softness of his skin. The fact that it is "carved" speaks of the beauty she sees in him. Such carvings usually told stories, and his body speaks to her.

When she says it is "inlaid with sapphires," there is probably no particular physical part of his anatomy to which she is referring, but rather to its overall beauty. It is beautiful to her because it houses a man who loves her deeply and wonderfully.

3. *She delights in his legs.*

The picture is one of strength. His legs were not skinny sticks but "pillars of marble set on bases of fine gold." He walked with dignity and strength of character. He was worth much to her, and she could not picture him with lesser quality. She chose the best and most excellent of building materials. That's what his lifestyle and character were like, and she wanted the ladies of the court to know how much she appreciated these qualities in his life.

The point of this is so important to the relationship of husbands and wives. Solomon combines strength with beauty and value. That's what attracts a wife to her husband. He is precious and valuable because she can depend upon him: He has legs like pillars of marble set on bases of fine gold. A building depends on a strong support system, which includes a good foundation and walls (or pillars) strong enough to sustain the weight of the structure. Abishag sees Solomon in this way.

4. *She delights in his countenance.*

She says that his "countenance [appearance] is like Lebanon, excellent as the cedars."

Before the battles between Moslems and Christians in recent years destroyed the country of Lebanon, it was ranked as one of the most beautiful countries in the world. It was our privilege to travel through the mountains, valleys, and coastal areas of this little country several years ago. What a delight that was, and what fantastic beauty in those "cedars of Lebanon"! The smell alone was captivating.

Abishag is summarizing the overall appearance of Solomon and connecting it with the beauty of Lebanon. He is like the most beautiful spot in the world!

She displays her true feelings for him.

His mouth is most sweet, yes,
he is altogether lovely. This is my beloved,
and this is my friend, O daughters of Jerusalem!

What a beautiful way to end her answer to these ladies of the court! She makes reference to three things about him that she finds most inviting.

1. *His communication is sweet.*

To say that his mouth was "most sweet" is to say how delightful it was to hear him speak. The word "mouth" refers to the palate or the source of speech (not to the lips or to kisses).

Nothing so attracts a wife to her husband as sweet communication. The way a man talks with his wife greatly affects her response to him. Observe again how Solomon speaks to this woman in the Song of Solomon. He was so complimentary and encouraging. His words were filled with love and tenderness. Husbands need to speak sweetly and kindly, not with bitterness or hostility (Colossians 3:19).

The words "most sweet" in Hebrew are plural. It means he was really sweet, doubly so!

2. *His character is attractive.*

She says he is "altogether lovely." Again, the word "lovely" is plural. It intensifies what she is saying. That's why the King James Version translates it "altogether" lovely. He is more than just lovely; he is lovely in every way!

Husbands, can your wives say that about you? Are you lovely in every way? Is everything about you a delight to your wife?

3. *His companionship is exciting.*

She calls him "my beloved," referring to the fact that he was her sexual partner and lover. She also calls him "my friend," a word indicating an intimate companion, someone much more than a sexual partner.

No word touches the heart of a wife so much as the word "friend." She wants to believe that her husband is her best friend. She wants to know that she can share anything and everything with him without being judged or attacked. She wants his counsel and encouragement. She needs to know what he thinks about what she says, feels, and does.

Solomon was attractive to Abishag in many ways, but perhaps this one verse summarizes it all. Sweet communication and intimate friendship dominated her thoughts of him. No wonder she spoke of him as "altogether lovely"!

A WORD FROM DAVID

My messages on the Song of Solomon are recorded on audiocassettes as well as videocassettes. When I delivered the message on Abishag's description of Solomon from this passage in chapter 5, Carole came up to the platform and read these words to me. It came from her heart and touched me greatly as she read so sweetly and lovingly. Watching her do this on videocassette was a second blessing to me. After she finished her reading I gave her a hug and kiss, and she took her seat.

As I preached that night, there was a great sense of joy in my heart because of Carole's presence and commitment to me. She is my friend. According to her, that's what she likes about me: I am her friend. Best and intimate friends are what every couple should be. That's what makes us "altogether lovely"!

Why He's So Special

SONG OF SOLOMON • 6:1-13

---

*He had no hesitation; he loved her
with all his heart and was not embarrassed to let
everyone know that she was his bride and lover!*

---

*A*bishag's dream in chapter 5 revealed the need to resolve sexual problems that arise within the marriage relationship. She asked the daughters of Jerusalem to help her find Solomon. They then questioned her as to why she wanted their help and why she thought Solomon was better than anyone else. She answered them in the last part of chapter 5 but now faces their penetrating question "Where has he gone?" They wanted to know why they should be asked to find him. Why would he leave her in the first place?

It may be only a dream and a hypothetical situation, but it was real in the emotions of Abishag. She now describes in great detail why Solomon is so special in her heart and life. It is an important passage for all wives to understand. Your husband needs praise and encouragement from you! He needs to know how much you love him and how special he is to your heart.

RESTORING THE RELATIONSHIP

*Where has your beloved gone,
O fairest among women? Where has your beloved
turned aside, that we may seek him with you?*

There is some question about the attitude of these ladies of the court. As we suggested in 5:9, their words "O fairest among women" may have been said with satire and mockery. If Solomon thinks she is the most beautiful of all women, why did he leave her? Why is she so earnestly seeking him now?

All of this started when Abishag refused to get out of bed and open her bedchamber door to her husband and lover. She now realizes her mistake. It is up to her to restore the relationship with Solomon that was strained through her reluctance to have sex with him.

Marriage can be tense at times for the dumbest reasons. The most trivial matter can become a giant barrier to our communication and our love for each other. We feel stupid when we think about our oversensitive responses, and how easy it is for us to make mountains out of molehills. But it happens.

REMEMBERING THE COMMITMENT

If marital difficulties are going to be resolved, we must remember our commitment to each other. It is "for better or for worse," we said in our vows. We like the "better." It's tough to endure the "worse."

There were two things involved in the commitment that

these two lovers made on their wedding day. One involved the responsibilities which Solomon would have as the king of Israel. Verse 2 reflects this when Abishag says:

> *My beloved has gone to his garden,*
> *to the beds of spices, to feed his flock*
> *in the gardens, and to gather lilies.*

That's romantic language for "he's got work to do!" That's a part of marital understanding. His commitment to her did not mean that he could forsake his responsibilities as king. Affairs of state had taken him away that night she refused to respond (chapter 5). Yes, he came home pretty late, but wasn't that her understanding when they got married? Will she be jealous that he must "feed his flock"?

Secondly, she remembers that their commitment to each other involved a strong relationship that could not be shaken by the business of the court or relationships with other people in the kingdom. She adds in 6:3:

> *I am my beloved's, and my beloved is mine.*
> *He feeds his flock among the lilies.*

The order is reversed here from what it was in 2:16. There she said, "My beloved is mine, and I am his." Why the change? She needs to express her commitment to him at this point in their marriage. She needs to let him know that she is committed to him no matter what duties will take him away from her at times. It is her way of apologizing to him for what happened when she refused to make love with him that night he came home late.

Do you get a little resentful when other people take your partner's time and energies? Believe us when we tell you that this can often happen in a preacher's home! A pastor's wife often gets "leftovers" in terms of her husband's time and emotions. He shares with so many people throughout the week that it becomes difficult for him to spend quality time with his wife. He is emotionally drained when he gets home.

We decided to solve this problem in our marriage by devoting one day a week to each other. When our children were small, we got a babysitter. When they were school-aged, we took them to school on that special day, spent the hours of the day with each other, and then picked them up again after school was out. We still try to spend that one day a week together. It is crucial to our marriage commitment and communication.

We also try to include special times together (in addition to our one day a week) by having breakfast or lunch with each other. Our marriage could not be what it is today without this quality time together. Our feelings are openly shared and our goals are discussed, for our children as well as for ourselves.

PRAISE INSTEAD OF CRITICISM

The insights of this particular section of the Song of Solomon are powerful. Solomon is special to Abishag because of the way he talks to her. He praises her continually rather than criticizing her. Even under the title of "constructive criticism" much damage is done.

Mary Ann was one depressed housewife! She reflected often in private conversation with others that she could not do anything right. She downgraded herself constantly, and people found it hard to be around her. The problem? A husband who criticized her and felt that this was his duty. He was trying to improve her and change her. This is what he thought was meant by "spiritual leadership."

When her husband, Robert, was confronted by a Christian friend, he expressed great surprise. His friend told him that the problem with his wife was that he was criticizing her instead of praising her. Robert did not like the implication that he was responsible for his wife's poor self-image and severe times of depression. He argued against such an opinion for several months.

Finally, during a message on the importance of a husband praising his wife (from Proverbs 31), Robert began to see what he was doing and how it was affecting his wife. Fortunately, this man was able to change, and the result in his wife's life has been utterly amazing to behold. She is a new woman with new confidence in the Lord and in what she is able to do with the Lord's help and power.

He praises her ability to overwhelm his emotions.

Solomon praises his wife in a way that would cause any woman to get excited. He speaks of how she affects him. He says in 6:4 that he was affected whenever he looked at her because she was so beautiful.

> *O my love, you are as beautiful as Tirzah,*
> *lovely as Jerusalem,*
> *awesome as an army with banners!*

Tirzah is mentioned in 1 Kings 16:8,15,17,23. It was known for its great natural beauty and had extensive gardens. It also had an abundant water supply. Abishag had natural beauty that reminded Solomon of one of the most beautiful cities in Israel, a place where the king would love to relax and enjoy the gorgeous surroundings.

Psalm 48:1,2 says of Jerusalem:

> *Great is the Lord, and greatly to be praised*
> *in the city of our God, in His holy mountain.*
> *Beautiful in elevation, the joy of the whole earth,*
> *is Mount Zion on the sides of the north,*
> *the city of the great King.*

There is a great beauty in the city of Jerusalem, even when one looks at its ruins. Standing on the eastern side of Jerusalem on the Mount of Olives and looking west toward the city, one senses its beauty and is affected emotionally by its history and by God's statements about it.

The phrase "awesome as an army with banners" could be translated "splendid to look upon." Solomon was struck emotionally with her loveliness, and his praise of her beauty had a deep effect upon him emotionally.

He was affected when he looked at her natural beauty, but was also affected when she looked at him. He said in 6:5:

> *Turn your eyes away from me,*
> *for they have overcome me.*

The New International Version says "overwhelm" and the New American Standard Bible uses the word "confused." This woman really touched him emotionally just by looking at him!

When love is in our hearts for each other, that's what just one look of the eyes can do. How powerful it is, and how wonderful to experience it! Can you say that about your spouse?

He praises her appearance as he saw it on their wedding night.

> *Your hair is like a flock of goats going down*
> *from Gilead. Your teeth are like a flock of sheep*
> *which have come up from the washing;*
> *every one bears twins, and none is barren*
> *among them. Like a piece of pomegranate*
> *are your temples behind your veil.*

Solomon reviews in brief form his earlier words to her on their wedding night. Another way of interpreting what he says is that nothing has changed—he still sees her as he saw her then.

He left out the references to her breasts and lips. Perhaps the reason he did this was so that she would not think he was just interested in sex. He wanted her friendship as well as her sexual love.

He praises her attractiveness above all others.

"Honey, you're the best!" These are words that every wife needs to hear from time to time. Solomon refers to at least four things at this point in his praise of Abishag.

1. *He refers to her prominence above all other women.*

> *There are sixty queens and eighty concubines,*
> *and virgins without number.*

The text does not say that Solomon had these women at this time. It is not "I have" but "there are." We believe that this is a poetic device, not an accurate count of his harem. The technique used here is "sixty, eighty, without number!" There may well have been more than 60 queens in the world, and there were certainly more than 80 concubines. This is simply a poetic device to emphasize that his wife, Abishag, is better than all the queens and concubines and virgins of the world!

2. *He refers to her place in her mother's heart.*

> *My dove, my perfect one, is the only one,*
> *the only one of her mother,*
> *the favorite of the one who bore her.*

The New International Version uses the word "unique." Solomon is pointing out that he is not the only one who sees how special his wife is—even her mother agrees! We might say in passing that it is a good thing to have the husband and his mother-in-law agreeing about things!

3. *He refers to the praise of other people.*

> *The daughters saw her and called her blessed,*
> *the queens and the concubines,*
> *and they praised her.*

The word "blessed" (Hebrew *asar*) carries the idea of "happy" or "congratulations." When the ladies of the court saw Abishag and the look on her face and the love in her heart for Solomon, they knew she was happy and one to be congratulated. Some people go through life and never have such joy.

They praised her (our English word "hallelujah") because they saw the qualities in her life that attracted Solomon. They knew he could have any woman in the world he wanted, but he chose Abishag. They praised her because Solomon praised her. He made her special in their eyes.

It's always a good idea for husbands to let other women know how much their wives mean to them. It helps eliminate attempts to undermine the marital bond. When a husband talks about his wife with criticism to another woman, he is setting himself up for a possible fall. Many affairs have begun by husbands indicating to other women how their wives were not ministering to them. Appealing to the sympathy and emotional understanding of another woman as it relates to your wife's inadequacies or weaknesses is dangerous business!

4. *He refers to the power of her attractiveness upon him.*

Who is she who looks forth as the morning,
fair as the moon, clear as the sun,
awesome as an army with banners?

The word for "moon" refers to a "full moon," usually a symbol of romantic moments. The word "clear" refers to something that is "bright." The New International Version says that she is "bright as the sun." She is beautiful and radiant. The reference to being "awesome as an army with banners" is repeated from 6:4 and can be translated "splendid to look upon."

Let's face it—this man is in love! Abishag has captured the heart of Solomon, and he finds her irresistible! What woman would not consider such a husband special? His praise of her (instead of criticism) attracted her greatly to him.

ROMANTIC REFLECTIONS

I went down to the garden of nuts to see the verdure of the valley, to see whether the vine had budded and the pomegranates had bloomed. Before I was even aware, my soul had made me as the chariots of my noble people.

Verse 11 reveals that she has some anxiety about how Solomon is going to respond to her after her refusal to make love with him (in her dream). The language here is poetic, and is symbolic of one who is not sure whether Solomon's love has "budded" and "bloomed" in its response. Will he hold this against her? Will he still be romantic toward her? These questions loom in her mind and heart as she emotionally walks through them, wondering how he will respond to her in the light of what happened.

Our relationships need reassurance from time to time. Tensions between husband and wife can cause insecurity, no matter how long you have been married. No one wants to be shut out and rejected.

The beautiful thing about this love story is how Abishag discovered the depth of Solomon's love and forgiveness. The New International Version in verse 12 reads, "Before I realized it, my desire set me among the royal chariots of my people." She experienced in the depths of her soul an awareness of the place she had in Solomon's heart. She was his queen, riding in the royal chariots, honored before all the people of his realm. He had no hesitation; he loved her with all his heart and was not embarrassed to let everyone know that she was his bride and lover!

LOVE AND DESIRE

Return, return, O Shulamite; return,
return, that we may look upon you!

Who speaks these words, urging Abishag to come back to Solomon's loving arms? Perhaps the ladies of the court are the only ones urging her to come back, but we think Solomon must also be one of the speakers, if not the principal one. The New King James Version indicates this fact when it places the title above these words "The Beloved and His Friends."

Abishag replies with this interesting but difficult-to-translate statement:

What would you see in the Shulamite—
as it were, the dance of the double camp?

The word "Shulamite" is the feminine form of the word "Solomon." What a wonderful encouragement it must have been to Abishag to be referred to in this way! It was like saying "You belong to me; you're a part of my life, and I'm incomplete without you!" Applying this to our lives, it's the same as saying that the term "David Hocking" is not complete without "Mrs. David Hocking" (Carole).

THE DANCE OF THE DOUBLE CAMP

What is the "dance of the double camp"? This is not an easy question to answer. The Hebrew words are *micholath ha-machanaim*. The first word means "dance," and might be referring to a passage like Jeremiah 31:3,4, which speaks of the dance of virgins. It was an ancient custom for the virgin bride to dance romantically and alluringly in front of her bridegroom. It was a sign of celebration, rejoicing, marriage, sexual love, etc.

The word *machanaim* is used for the small town where

Jacob saw the angels of God. It was a "double camp" to Jacob, for not only did he camp there, but so did a company of angels. This same word appears in Genesis 32:7,10, when Jacob divided his people and possessions into "two companies." The word appears over 200 times in the Old Testament, and refers to a camp, company, host, troops, armies, etc.

Perhaps Abishag is asking whether Solomon's desire to look at her means that he sees her like an angel from heaven. It may be that she is asking whether Solomon wants to look at her in private or in front of others. Is it a dance of the "double camp"—in front of Solomon as well as the ladies of the court? She is asking this to determine whether this is really the romantic desire of Solomon. It would make a difference to her if it was simply the urging of the ladies of the court but did not represent the romantic love of Solomon.

It is difficult to know how to interpret her response. The Hebrew and Greek texts of this passage place this verse at the beginning of chapter 7 rather than at the end of chapter 6. That's important to understand. Chapter 7 is Solomon's romantic and sensual description of Abishag, and it appears from the way this passage reads that she is dancing in front of him in a very sensuous and alluring manner.

Some interpreters believe that the simplest way to take her response is to view her as saying, "Why do you want to look at me when there are so many others in the dance?" By what takes place in chapter 7, this makes sense. Abishag wants to know if Solomon is still as sexually motivated toward her as he was on their wedding night.

Many marriages have lost the romance and sexual desires of the wedding night. The relationship becomes routine, even dull. There is a lack of romantic communication and physical affection outside the bedroom. Sex becomes duty and expectation rather than joy and excitement. But God's love can change such a situation! God's love can put romance back into hearts that have grown cold and indifferent.

13 | A Sensuous Look

The Bible approves of sexual pleasure and enjoyment, and describes physical intimacy between husband and wife with no reservation or inhibition.

Writers on the Song of Solomon speak of this chapter as the most sensuous of all. They call it "explicit" and "erotic." One writer says that Abishag has "no problems with inhibitions" in this passage. Another says it is "sensual and intimate."

The scene is the private bedchamber of Solomon and Abishag. She has removed her clothes and is dancing sensuously in front of her lover and husband. The moment is special, romantic, sensual, intimate, private, and needed.

In chapter 4 Solomon listed seven qualities of his beautiful bride; in this chapter he describes ten. Both numbers speak of perfection and completion. The Ten Commandments summarize God's holy and righteous character, His moral standards. Solomon describes his wife with ten qualities. Going from seven to ten seems to imply a growth in familiarity and intimacy. There is more now that captures his attention than what he saw on their wedding night. That's the way it should be in every marriage as we grow in love for each other.

DESCRIBING THE BEAUTY

Solomon is entranced by the movements of her dance. He starts at her feet and moves slowly up her body, ending with her hair. In chapter 4 he started at the top, describing the beauties of her face, and ended with her breasts. He went no farther. But here in chapter 7 he becomes more descriptive and more intimate.

1. *He describes her feet.*

> *How beautiful are your feet in sandals,*
> *O prince's daughter!*

The word "beautiful" carries the idea of being graceful, and matches with the facts of this passage which indicate that she is dancing in front of him. He sees the movement of her feet as a beautiful and alluring act. The reference to her feet may also be describing the steps of the dance.

2. *He describes her thighs.*

> *The curves of your thighs are like jewels,*
> *the work of the hands of a skillful workman.*

The "curves of your thighs" may be referring to the movement of them during the dance. The New American Standard Bible changes "thighs" to "hips," and the New International Version translates "Your graceful legs are like jewels."

This word for "thighs" is also found in 3:8, where the 60 valiant men of Solomon had swords strapped to their thighs.

It would seem that the area from the waist down, including the hips, is the meaning of the word. The word "curves" suggests the circular motion of her hips and legs as she dances in front of him.

Her hips are so beautiful to his eyes that he concludes they must have been designed by a very skillful workman. Indeed they were—the hands of God Himself!

While not always understandable to wives, husbands have a great interest and sexual desire toward a woman's hips and legs. Moving them or displaying them in a sensuous manner can be very sexually motivating to a man. Solomon is obviously motivated here in this passage as he views the way his wife is dancing before him, clearly trying to please him and draw him to her in order to make love once again.

3. *He describes her navel.*

> *Your navel is a rounded goblet*
> *which lacks no blended beverage.*

The word translated "navel" is used in Ezekiel 16:4 to refer to the umbilical cord. This word may also refer to the female genitals, and this could make sense in light of the order in which Solomon is describing his wife. He starts at her feet and moves up her body. Since the waist comes next, followed by the breasts, we wonder whether this refers to the navel. A more likely place is the female genitals.

The "rounded goblet" is referring to a bowl-shaped glass pictured as a half-moon. This symbolism fits better if it refers to her genitals rather than her navel. The fact that it contains mixed, spiced, or blended wine makes it a symbol of sexual pleasure (cf. 5:1), and tends to confirm the idea that her sexual organs are being described.

One thing should be clear from this sensuous description: No part of our body is to be considered unattractive or off-limits within the bond of marriage. The Bible approves of sexual pleasure and enjoyment, and describes physical intimacy between husband and wife with no reservation or inhibition.

The young wife who talked with us was disturbed about her husband's "perverted desires." She said that he enjoyed seeing her without her clothes on (and she didn't mind that), but she was shocked to discover how much he wanted to "examine" her and "touch" her. It seems that her mother had instilled within her some erroneous concepts about what is right within the bond of marriage. Through some careful study of the Song of Solomon, her heart was changed, and today her husband is most grateful!

4. *He describes her waist.*

> *Your waist is a heap of wheat*
> *set about with lilies.*

Solomon continues to move up her body. He pauses at her waist and comes out with a description that sounds strange to our modern ears. A "heap of wheat" refers to that which is prepared for a meal and is quite soft. The Hebrew grammar technically refers to the lower abdomen, below the navel. It is used for the womb and the fetus being carried there. He is not describing the imaginary line above the hips where most women wear a belt. He is referring to the lower abdomen, immediately above the female genitals, and pictures it as being beautiful, graceful, tender, and soft.

At this point something needs to be said to all married couples. There are times when a person is heavy but still attractive, but most of us realize that it is not only bad for our health to be overweight but not very attractive to our spouse. The discipline and commitment necessary to lose weight is an awesome responsibility and a difficult experience.

The truth is that we all have a better feeling about ourselves when we lose a few pounds, and this helps us to relate better to our spouses, and they to us.

5. *He describes her breasts.*

Your two breasts are like two fawns,
twins of a gazelle.

This same description was used by Solomon in 4:5. It is
a picture of two soft, graceful, and tender animals, somewhat
like deer. They are desirable to touch and caress, and that's
how Solomon felt about Abishag's breasts. He loved to hold
them, but with tenderness. He enjoyed feeling them, but he
did it gently and lovingly. Good advice for every husband!
  6. *He describes her neck.*

Your neck is like an ivory tower.

Her neck was smooth like ivory and long like a tower,
picturing strength of character and integrity.
  The female neck is attractive to men. They love to put their
hands around it and feel its softness and strength. When the
neck is adorned with a beautiful chain or necklace, it seems
to enhance the beauty. The neck connects the head to the body
and is an important part of a woman's overall beauty.
  But without integrity in the heart of a woman, the neck
loses its beauty. How important it is in the midst of all these
sensual and physical descriptions to understand the
relationship of it all to the inward spirit and heart of the
person! What you are inside affects the beauty which other
people see on the outside.
  7. *He describes her eyes.*

Your eyes [are] like the pools in Heshbon
by the gate of Bath Rabbim.

Excavations have revealed the remains of large reservoirs
near the city of Heshbon. "Pools" indicate that which is
peaceful and gentle. The Hebrew words "Bath Rabbim" mean
"daughter of many." The idea is that the peacefulness of

Abishag's eyes is to be contrasted with a populous city having congestion, traffic, and busyness.

Solomon finds in Abishag a quiet retreat; he sees it in her eyes. When he looks at her he feels relaxed and refreshed, like the "pools of Heshbon."

8. *He describes her nose.*

> *Your nose is like the tower of Lebanon*
> *which looks toward Damascus.*

The word "Lebanon" means "white." Looking toward Damascus, one sees limestone cliffs on the eastern slopes of Lebanon's mountains. When the sun shines on them they look white in appearance, and so the name "Lebanon."

The symbolism of a tower emphasizes her strong character. A tower's purpose was to protect the people by providing an alert for any approach of an enemy. Her nose reminded him of how she was a protection to him.

Noses are not often used in the romantic literature of Western culture to compliment a person, but in the Middle East it was common. The nose was a symbol of beauty and dignity, and was attractive in its own special way.

9. *He describes her head.*

> *Your head crowns you like Mount Carmel.*

What a beautiful statement! Mount Carmel sits like a crown on the head of the city of Haifa. It is beautiful and impressive. Solomon took one look at Abishag and thought of that beautiful scene on the shores of the Mediterranean Sea.

He is saying that she needs no other crown (though she was now the queen) than the beauty of her own head. How encouraging he was to her, always aware of her insecurity stemming from her background—after all, she was just a "country girl."

10. *He describes her hair.*

*The hair of your head is like purple;
the king is held captive by its tresses.*

The New American Standard Bible sees the strands of the hair as "purple threads." Some see a picture of royalty here. The strands of her hair had captured the heart of Solomon, and running his fingers through it or laying his face within those strands was all that was necessary for him to fix his heart upon her.

A woman's hair is her glory (1 Corinthians 11:15). Shaving a woman's hair is described as "shame." It humiliates her and reduces her sense of womanhood and attractiveness. Women who cut their hair as short as men in order to be masculine in appearance or attitude are making a gigantic mistake. God intends for the hair of a woman to be longer than her husband's hair. God wants us to maintain sexual distinctions between male and female because this affects sexual attraction and sexual roles and relationships.

There is nothing wrong with going to the beauty shop or having your hair cut and trimmed or designed. The principle deals with the relationship of a woman's hair to her husband's. Is there a clear distinction between them? Is her hair longer than his? Does the wife understand that her hair is her glory, a mark of her femininity, an attraction to her husband?

What will happen next?

Abishag has been dancing in front of Solomon in their private bedchamber. Solomon describes her from foot to head, especially dwelling on her sensual attractiveness. Does it all end here? Of course not. Solomon becomes more direct now, and indicates that he is ready to make love with her. She will then respond and give him her love.

ENJOYING THE PHYSICAL AFFECTION

One of the interesting things about the Song of Solomon

is the verbal interchange that goes on during the process of making love. Solomon tells her what he is going to do. He seems to build her anticipation, and she longs for him to do it. That's important for every husband and wife to understand.

One of the great needs in marriage relationships is to emphasize the role of the husband in preparing his wife for lovemaking. Husbands are ready before wives are emotionally prepared. One of the best ways for husbands to prepare their wives and to demonstrate their love for them and their needs is to give constant words of praise. To describe your wife's physical attractiveness to you is a key to her response to you.

He describes the enjoyment he saw in her.

> *How fair and how pleasant you are,*
> *O love, with your delights!*

The word "delights" is translated "charms" by the New American Standard Bible. The word refers to that which is luxurious and erotic. Solomon had seen her beauty ("fair") and her charm ("pleasant") before, but here he connects it with her sexuality ("delights"). She was indeed a joy to his heart and was filled with enjoyment for him to experience.

He describes the enticement he felt.

> *This stature of yours is like a palm tree,*
> *and your breasts like its clusters. I said,*
> *"I will go up to the palm tree, I will take hold*
> *of its branches." Let now your breasts*
> *be like clusters of the vine.*

When a farmer harvested dates, he would climb the palm tree with his legs and arms wrapped around its trunk. It was an effort, but the reward was well worth it. He compares her breasts with the clusters of both dates and grapes. Both are fruits connected with sexual pleasure. Both are sweet to the taste.

Solomon is speaking of more than fondling her breasts with his hands; he is speaking of tasting them. He has increased the sensuality of his communication and is clearly telling her that he is ready to make love with her.

He describes the effect of her love.

The fragrance of your breath like apples,
and the roof of your mouth like the best wine.

The word translated "breath" is the Hebrew word "nose." Some commentators believe that it is a reference to the nipples of her breasts. The smell of her breasts was like the sweetness of delicious fruit. Her breasts with their nipples were having a powerful effect upon his desires at this point.

The statement about the "roof of your mouth" is speaking about her kisses and primarily focusing on taste. Her kisses to him were like the best wine, bringing so much joy to his heart, a feeling of ecstasy and celebration.

There is no doubt about the sensuality of these words from the lips of Solomon. He is more than ready! How will Abishag respond?

DESIRING TRUE LOVE

The wine goes down smoothly for my beloved,
moving gently the lips of sleepers.
I am my beloved's, and his desire is toward me.

Three things are involved here in the response of Abishag to Solomon's words of love. She sees it as a *celebration*. She says, "The wine goes down smoothly for my beloved." There is no hesitancy here on her part, no reluctance to give all to him. She is ready, and indicates that the sexual pleasure they will enjoy together will be totally satisfying to them both ("goes down smoothly").

Secondly, she knows it brings *contentment*. When she says, "moving gently the lips of sleepers," she speaks of falling asleep together after lovemaking—with complete satisfaction! What a loving and beautiful response!

Finally, she emphasizes the matter of *commitment*. She says, "I am my beloved's, and his desire is toward me." Commitment to each other in marriage produces the greatest level of sexual satisfaction and contentment. It creates the environment in which sexual pleasure can be enjoyed without regret or hesitation.

THREE STAGES OF COMMITMENT

1. Song of Solomon 2:16—"*My beloved is mine, and I am his.*"

When they were courting each other, there was a need for *security*. There was indecision about their relationship and possible marriage. That had to be resolved. It takes commitment to do so.

2. Song of Solomon 6:3—"*I am my beloved's, and my beloved is mine.*"

After the marriage, Abishag's dream pointed out the importance of meeting each other's needs, no matter how late her husband came home from his duties as king. There was a need for *submission*, a willingness to give to the other partner regardless of how you feel. Her indifference to his desires was the problem. It takes commitment to solve this problem as well.

3. Song of Solomon 7:10—"*I am my beloved's, and his desire is toward me.*"

Abishag was insecure about Solomon's love for her after she withdrew from him when he desired her. Will their relationship ever again be satisfactory and acceptable to him? She had her doubts and questions. Commitment was needed here also in order to bring *stability* back to their relationship.

Her words in 7:10 clearly show that she is now convinced: "He still loves me, and is totally committed to me."

The greatest need in our marriages is commitment—a commitment involving security, submission, and stability. Our marriage vows state it well: "Until death parts us."

14 | *I Will Give You My Love*

This is sex from God's point of view—explicit and intimate, filled with pleasure and enjoyment. There has never been a more beautiful description nor a more complete picture of marital love.

*I*n this lovely passage Abishag does the talking and the inviting. After all, Solomon has been describing her physical attractiveness and sexual delights. He is ready, and according to the verses just preceding this section, so is she. She's ready to celebrate with him.

THE SECLUDED RESORT

Come, my beloved, let us go forth to the field; let us lodge in the villages. Let us get up early to the vineyards; let us see if the vine has budded, whether the grape blossoms are open,

and the pomegranates are in bloom.
There I will give you my love.

The words "there I will give you my love" emphasize that she is looking for a romantic and secluded spot to enjoy their lovemaking. There are two reasons for this:

1. The need for privacy and a change in environment.
2. The need for renewal and romance.

Carole and I enjoy immensely a couple of days away. It doesn't really matter where they are as long as they are "away"! We enjoy sex at home, of course, but taking a few days off and getting away from the normal routine and duties is necessary at times. A change in environment can do wonders for a couple struggling in their sexual relationship with each other. It is so helpful in terms of communication. With the children around, we don't always have the time or the intimacy we want.

When Abishag speaks of whether the "vine has budded" she is talking about their relationship, not simply a study of grapes. If the "grape blossoms are open" and "the pomegranates are in bloom," then everything is great—their relationship is flourishing and their love for each other is strong.

Are the "buds, blossoms, and blooms" in your life what they should be? When was the last time you went as a couple (without your children) to a secluded spot in order to enjoy your love? Is your marriage filled with romance these days, or could you stand a little improvement?

One of our fond memories relates to the night we went out to dinner and then to the Laguna Arts Festival. Carole thought we would be going back home that night, but David had arranged a hotel room on the beach, and we spent the night together. Some might say, "A bed is a bed," thinking that getting away is not all that important. We know differently. The romance of that night still lingers in our memory. What a special time it was for renewal and romance! Stop making excuses—we all need these times of privacy and romance.

PLANNING THE RELATIONSHIP

Abishag is going to respond to Solomon's desires for her. She has some special plans in mind, and he is going to enjoy it immensely! This sexual relationship that she has planned for him involves four things.

1. *It involves her creativity.*

> *The mandrakes give off a fragrance,*
> *and at our gates are pleasant fruits,*
> *all manner, new and old.*

Mandrakes were considered an aphrodisiac. The Arabs called them "the servant of love." She is indicating to Solomon that she has some surprises for him when she says "At our gates are pleasant fruits, all manner, new and old." She is going to be creative in how she responds to him, and that is enjoyable to any husband.

Creativity means different things to different people. Some wives choose to be creative in how they dress (or undress). The point in this passage deals with sexual affection and response. What surprises can a wife bring to her husband, especially when they have been married for several years? Sometimes it simply means to make love in a different place or in a different way. Variety is so important in keeping our relationship alive and fresh.

Wives, the important thing to understand is the need of your husbands for your creativity. One look at him may convince you otherwise, but don't believe it! No matter how dull or boring you think he is, your sexual responses are needed and desired. Be creative. Hold his hand when he doesn't expect it; rub his neck and shoulders at a time and place that would surprise him; put your arm around him when you don't normally do that in a given situation; give him some creative kisses of love at moments he least expects them. Creativity is important to your relationship, and love is willing and responsive to things "new and old."

2. *It involves her loyalty.*

Which I have laid up for you, my beloved.

Sex without loyalty is demeaning and unfulfilling. Abishag knows better. She has saved all these surprises and sexual delights just for Solomon—no one else. That's what makes their sexual relationship with each other so special. Wives need to express that kind of devotion to their husbands as surely as husbands need to do that for their wives. The special loyalty of a wife that gives to her husband what no other man will receive is indeed attractive to him.

3. *It involves her ability.*

Oh, that you were like my brother,
who nursed at my mother's breasts! If I should
find you outside, I would kiss you;
I would not be despised. I would lead you
and bring you into the house of my mother,
she who used to instruct me.

She refers to Solomon as her brother, who was nursed by her mother's breasts. She is inviting Solomon to enjoy her breasts as well as indicating that she wants him to depend upon her like her brother did when he was being nursed by her mother.

She indicated that she has the ability to show him affection as well as to understand his need. Kissing in a sexual way out in public pictures a harlot (Proverbs 7:10-23) and not a godly woman. What she is saying is that she is so committed to Solomon that she would do this and not be despised because everyone would know how loyal she is to him.

That's good advice for all of us. The best way to avoid suspicion and eliminate any doubts that people may have about your sexual commitment is to make sure they know how much you love your spouse! When that is weak or questionable—watch out!

Abishag's words "I would lead you and bring you into the house of my mother, she who used to instruct me" indicate that she wants Solomon to become her teacher now. Her mother instructed her in how to love her husband, but now she wants Solomon to teach her. That's wisdom! Any husband would be excited to hear that from his wife!

The "house of her mother" may be the same as in 3:4, where we read "until I had brought him to the house of my mother, and into the chamber of her who conceived me." She is talking about the bedroom.

4. *It involves her desirability.*

I would cause you to drink of spiced wine,
of the juice of my pomegranate.

What she is saying by these words is, "You're really going to enjoy it!" Abishag has no hesitation in letting Solomon know how excited she is about making love with him, and how enjoyable he will find it to be.

The words "spiced wine" indicate that she will be so desirable that he will become intoxicated with her love and desire for him. The "juice of my pomegranate" reminds us of chapter 4, where Solomon described her sexuality as "an orchard of pomegranates with pleasant fruits" (verse 13). Abishag spoke in 4:16 about her sexuality and said, "Blow upon my garden, that its spices may flow out." She is picturing her sexuality as juices and fruits for him to enjoy. Here, in

8:2, she says that she will cause him to drink of her wine and juice. She wants to give him her love, and says that he will thoroughly enjoy it. That thought brings her great delight.

Proverbs 5:18,19 agrees when it says:

*Let your fountain be blessed, and rejoice with the
wife of your youth. As a loving deer and a
graceful doe, let her breasts satisfy you at all
times; and always be enraptured with her love.*

The word "enraptured" means "intoxicated." The romantic language here is similar to that of the Song of Solomon. Sexual pleasure is approved by biblical teaching and encouraged by the explicit material found in the Song of all songs.

ANTICIPATING THE RESPONSE

*His left hand is under my head,
and his right hand embraces me.*

These same words were found in 2:6. As we mentioned earlier, this statement is not a formula or suggested position. He looks directly at her and with his right hand caresses her body and her sexual parts.

Abishag anticipates this beautiful sexual relationship with Solomon. She literally invited Solomon to enjoy her sexuality and promises to respond creatively to all he desires and needs.

This is sex from God's point of view—explicit and intimate, filled with pleasure and enjoyment. There has never been a more beautiful description nor a more complete picture of marital love. But within these words of sensual pleasure are warnings about premarital and extramarital sex. God is not against sexual pleasure. His sexual laws restricting this pleasure within marriage are not intended to keep us from having fun, but to protect us from damaging our emotional and physical well-being. He knows us better than we know ourselves.

A SERIOUS WARNING

I charge you, O daughters of Jerusalem,
do not stir up nor awaken love until it pleases.

We have met this instruction twice before in 2:7 and 3:5. It is a warning against premarital and extramarital sex. It is a statement about the uncontrollable nature of human passion. It fully agrees with the New Testament teaching (1 Corinthians 7:5), and cautions us about the power of sexual desire.

The three occasions in which this warning appears are not all in the same context. It appears that three distinct factors relate to the power of sexual desire. It is dangerous to arouse your sexual passion outside of the instruction and approval of God, for the following reasons:

1. Song of Solomon 2:7—*Because it hurts your ability to enjoy sex.*
2. Song of Solomon 3:5—*Because it hinders your objectivity and attitudes toward the one you will marry or the one to whom you are married.*
3. Song of Solomon 8:4—*Because it affects your ability to be romantic with your marital partner and to make necessary adjustments in marriage.*

Enjoyment, attitudes, and romance are all affected by premarital or extramarital sex. Sexual satisfaction and contentment as well as pleasure and enjoyment are related to fidelity. This does not mean that a person cannot enjoy a sexual relationship outside of marriage. There is often pleasure in sin, according to the Bible, but it does not last. The heart is not fulfilled and the mind is not satisfied.

Extramarital affairs do great damage to the emotional and mental capacities of our lives. God intended that we be loyal to one mate, and this means having sex with only our marital partner!

This teaching of Song of Solomon 2:7, 3:5, and 8:4 emphasizes the power of sexual desire. If we do not control it the way God intended, it will cause great problems within us as well as great hurts to others with whom we become involved. It is dangerous to let sexual desires be stirred up or awakened, for they are more powerful than we think. Many people have fallen into sexual immorality because they thought they could control sexual desire. God says we can't (1 Corinthians 7:5), and we had better listen!

What should you do when you feel sexual desire toward someone other than your spouse?

1. Don't conclude that the other person was meant to be your spouse simply because you feel sexual desire toward that person.
2. Don't encourage your sexual interest in another person by flirtation or inappropriate physical affection.
3. Immediately pray about it. God knows your need better than you do, so call upon Him for help.
4. Stay away from private times with that person; don't allow yourself to be alone with him or her.
5. Concentrate on your spouse and direct your sexual interest and desires toward him or her.
6. Contact your spouse right away, and if greatly pressured by your desires, make arrangements with your spouse to make love as soon as possible.
7. Determine in your heart to remain loyal and committed to your spouse. This means that you

refuse to have sex with anyone else, no matter how strong your desires or feelings of love.

The spiritual ingredients that help us gain the victory over our sinful desires include:

1. Prayer: Matthew 26:41.
2. The Bible: Psalm 119:9-11.
3. The Holy Spirit: Galatians 5:16.
4. Our spouse: 1 Corinthians 7:1-5.

Sexual desire is a beautiful thing that is given to us by God Himself. May God help us to control it within our marriage and to satisfy all our needs through His appointed means— our marital partner!

15 | *Why Love Is So Powerful*

SONG OF SOLOMON • 8:5-14

Most of us want to experience an overpowering love relationship with our spouse, but we simply do not know where to begin.

---

he Bible has much to say about love. First John 4:8 tells us that "God is love." He is not merely loving, but His *essential nature* is that of love. His love gives even when there is no response (Romans 5:8; 1 John 4:19), and it is a love rooted in sacrifice (1 John 3:16). The greatest moment of expressing His love was when Jesus Christ, His only Son, died on the cross for our sins (1 John 4:9,10; John 3:16).

Husbands are to love their wives like Jesus Christ loved the church and gave Himself up for her (Ephesians 5:25-27). They are to love their wives as they love their own bodies or as they love themselves (Ephesians 5:28,33).

The greatest definition of God's love is presented in 1

Corinthians 13:1-13, the love chapter in the Bible. There we learn of the marvelous qualities of God's love and how it never fails even though many gifts of God will cease to function in time. God's love is powerful and is a wonderful thing to experience, both in giving and receiving.

Arnold and his wife were having a hard time. They talked about divorce even though they were Christians. Arnold's wife felt no love, and Arnold wasn't sure he loved his wife anymore. On a vacation in Hawaii (a miserable time, according to them), they were ready to divorce. Both said those terrible words, "I don't love you anymore."

After getting back to their home in California, they started to make plans for a divorce. They called a Christian attorney who had the wisdom of God. He confronted them about the teachings of the Bible and told them that they could learn to love each other. They were surprised that an attorney would talk to them this way. He challenged them to read 1 Corinthians 13 every day for one month, and then he would discuss this matter of divorce with them.

About a week before they were to meet with the attorney, Arnold called him and said, "It won't be necessary for us to meet with you. The Bible has canceled our plans for divorce." He went on to say how the qualities of God's love in 1 Corinthians 13 began to change their feelings about each other. He said, "We are in love again, and divorce is no longer an option for us."

The closing verses of the Song of Solomon reveal four things upon which God's love is based in the marriage that operates according to divine instruction. These four essentials tell us why love is so powerful between a husband and a wife. Most of us want to experience an overpowering love relationship with our spouse, but we simply do not know where to begin. This passage gives specific help.

GOD'S LOVE IS BASED
ON SEXUAL CONTENTMENT

Verse 4 warns against awakening love and sexual passion outside of marriage. Verse 5 indicates that Solomon awakened the sexual love of Abishag.

Who is this coming up from the wilderness, leaning upon her beloved? I awakened you under the apple tree. There your mother brought you forth; there she who bore you brought you forth.

The picture of Abishag leaning upon Solomon after their sexual encounter of the previous verses is a beautiful statement on sexual contentment. She pictures one who is relaxed and fully satisfied with what took place. God's love brings that kind of sexual satisfaction and contentment.

Solomon refers to their sexual passion and paints the picture of it happening exactly in the same way that Abishag's mother and father experienced it. That's how Abishag came into this world. How happy the child who knows that he or she is the product of parents filled with God's love, enjoying sexual pleasure, experiencing great contentment with each other, and bearing a child because of it! That's how it happened with us, and we are so grateful to the Lord for it.

GOD'S LOVE IS BASED
ON STRONG COMMITMENT

A dear lady who listens to our daily radio broadcast in the Midwest gave us a beautifully framed picture which contains the words of these two verses in calligraphy. It means a great deal to us.

Set me as a seal upon your heart,
as a seal upon your arm; for love
is as strong as death, jealousy as cruel
as the grave; its flames are flames of fire,
a most vehement flame. Many waters
cannot quench love, nor can the floods drown it.
If a man would give for love all the wealth
of his house, it would be utterly despised.

No stronger words of commitment have ever been spoken! This commitment has four basic characteristics that every married couple should carefully evaluate.

1. *It is an INTIMATE commitment.*

Possession of another person's seal means that you have free access to all that he or she possesses. The heart is the source of affections and the arm is the source of strength. Abishag is laying claim to Solomon's heart and strength. She wants to be closer to his heart than anyone else. That is vitally important in order for a relationship to be what it should be.

Does anyone else have that place in your heart? Have you felt a stronger tie to someone other than your marital partner? If you have, your commitment to your spouse is weak and is vulnerable to temptation and future difficulties.

2. *It is an INTENSE commitment.*

When Abishag says that "love is as strong as death," these are words of strong commitment. They symbolize intensity in the relationship. Jealousy can be a good thing; God is a jealous God. The phrase "a most vehement flame" is often translated "the flame of Jehovah." Some hold that the last syllable of the Hebrew word is the shortened form of the name Jehovah. The point is that the "flame of Jehovah" would refer to love as a flame which has its origin in God.

However, the simplest way of taking this phrase is that it describes how intense love can be in terms of commitment. Death and the grave are graphic illustrations, for love has similar characteristics. It reminds us of songs that say God's love will never let us go. Love holds on for dear life. It is based on an intense commitment to your marital partner. Is that true of your heart?

When Deborah spoke of her husband, you could feel her hurt and disappointment. She was ready to give up. He was flirtatious with other women, especially at his office, and he seemed to ignore her a great deal when they were with other couples. After hearing a message on these verses, she decided that her commitment to him was not what it should be, and she determined to make it as intense as possible.

The first thing she did really surprised him. When he came home from the office, he found a sign on the front door which said, "No matter what you do, I will never leave you or forsake you!" He was honored and embarrassed at the same time. Interestingly, he knew right away what she was saying. According to him, he felt instant guilt about his actions with other women. He confessed it to her and told her how foolish he was and how much he loved her and was committed to her. Their marriage has been different ever since! Her sign may not work for you, but the point behind it is powerful: How intense is your commitment to your spouse?

3. *It is an INDESTRUCTIBLE commitment.*

"Many waters cannot quench love, nor can the floods drown it." What wonderful words! If you have God's love, then these facts are true. If your love is something less, these thoughts may not represent the level of your commitment.

Too many of us give up too easily. Our love fades under the pressure of difficult circumstances and feelings of rejection. But God's love remains no matter what kind of floods try to drown it. The pressures will come, but God's love can withstand it all.

When a friend's spouse committed adultery, she was heartbroken. Thoughts of divorce (and murder!) entered her mind. "How could he do this to me?" she asked. "Who does he think he is?" A wounded ego was obvious, and a desire for revenge frequently came out of her mouth.

We warned her about allowing her husband's infidelity to change her own commitment. But this "flood" was too much for her, and before we could help in any further way, she got involved with another man, divorced her husband, and married the man with whom she had the affair. She felt fully justified in doing it. How sad!

God's love is still around even after it has been severely hurt. God's love can cope with the most tragic circumstances and gets stronger through it all.

4. *It is an INVALUABLE commitment.*

Sex can be bought, but love must be given. If you try to give all the wealth you possess in order to buy God's love, it would be "utterly despised." Nothing compares with the power of God's love.

Some husbands try to buy their wife's love by giving her expensive material gifts. That's thoughtful, but not the way to experience God's love. God's love is built on stronger stuff than "things." It flows from the heart of God and does not give itself on the basis of the other person's performance. It is produced in our hearts by the Holy Spirit of God (Romans 5:5; Galatians 5:22), and it is not a commodity which can be bought and sold.

GOD'S LOVE IS BASED
ON PERSONAL CHARACTER

Personal character is crucial to commitment. When a person is not controlled by integrity, commitments are not kept and promises never fulfilled. You can make a vow to your husband or wife and say all the right words, but apart from moral character the vow is usually broken.

Insight into Abishag's character is given in these verses and continues to press home to our hearts the importance of what a person is inside. This is more essential to commitment than all the outward attractions of a beautiful body.

If we are not strong in our hearts, we are usually weak in our commitments. Inside, in the deepest recesses of our souls, is where the battle is fought. Commitment must come from the heart and be based upon moral integrity and sound character. Your reputation is what people think you are; your character is what God knows you to be.

Her character was developed in her family background.

We have a little sister, and she has no breasts.
What shall we do for our sister
in the day when she is spoken for?
If she is a wall, we will build upon her
a battlement of silver; and if she is a door,
we will enclose her with boards of cedar.

Abishag's brothers are speaking. We met them in 1:6. They did not always treat Abishag well, but they did have concern for her moral purity. When she was young and had no breasts, an evaluation was made. The family sensed their responsibility. The brothers concluded that if she was a "wall," then all they should do is enhance it with "a battlement of silver." They would simply make her more beautiful. Being a "wall" referred to her strength of character.

But if Abishag were easily seduced or seemed quite vulnerable as she grew up, then they would "enclose her with boards of cedar." Is she going to be a "door" or a "wall"? Will she be able to resist temptations that come her way, or will she give in to them?

The fact that the family was concerned about this shows us the importance of the family in terms of character development as well as protection. They sensed their responsibility to Abishag, and were willing to do what was necessary to preserve her moral integrity.

Her character was determined by her own choices.

I am a wall, and my breasts like towers;
then I became in his eyes as one who found peace.

Abishag is declaring her own maturity here and her read-
iness for marriage. The size and development of her breasts
is clearly the key. Her choice as a girl growing up was to be
"a wall," thus demonstrating that she had moral integrity
before she ever got married to Solomon.

Abishag is an example for every girl to follow. Solomon was
attracted by her moral purity. "In his eyes" she was a woman
of character who brought peace, not trouble, to his heart.

When Abishag refers to her breasts being "like towers,"
the emphasis is not on the size of her breasts, although their
development shows that she is ready to be married. The mention of "towers" indicates strength and protection. Abishag
has made a personal choice to remain pure until marriage,
and in spite of how alluring and attractive she was physically,
especially in terms of her breasts, she had moral integrity and
strength that made those lovely breasts seem like "towers"
symbolizing her personal character.

Several years ago a beautiful young lady shared with us
her disappointment over her relationships with boys who
called themselves Christians. She was attractive and had well-
developed breasts. She was obviously proud of the way she
looked. She told us how the boys would always take advantage
of her and would feel her breasts before the evening was over.

Somehow she did not seem convincing. As we questioned
a little more, we discovered that she lacked the commitment
of Abishag. She knew that the boys enjoyed looking at and
touching her breasts, and while she was outwardly complain-
ing because these relationships were not meaningful to her,
she enjoyed the effect which she had on the boys she dated.
We challenged her to moral integrity. She needed to make
the decision in her heart to refuse such activity and save
herself for the man she would one day marry.

Sadly, we must report that she did not listen. Before the
year was up, she was pregnant, and the years since have
brought her much sorrow. She has been divorced several
times and seemingly cannot find a meaningful relationship.

Her character was demonstrated in her response to Solomon.

Solomon had a vineyard in Baal Hamon;
he leased the vineyard to keepers; everyone
was to bring for its fruit a thousand pieces of silver.
My own vineyard is before me. You, O Solomon,
may have a thousand, and those who
keep its fruit two hundred.

These words have brought much confusion to Bible teachers. What is meant here by this "vineyard"?

It appears that Abishag compared the rights of Solomon to administer his own possessions and her right to her own person. Another way of putting it would be, "You've got a lot, Solomon, but I'm the best vineyard you have!"

The last words of verse 12 seem to be a request for Solomon to reward her brothers, who cared for her as she was growing up. It was customary to reward the keeper of your vineyards from the profits you received from their faithful endeavors. She is simply asking Solomon to recognize the value of what he has received in her as his bride, and to appreciate the role that her family played in making it all possible. This clearly shows what kind of person Abishag really was. She did not forget her family after she was brought to Solomon's palace and made his queen. That shows character.

GOD'S LOVE IS BASED
ON INTIMATE COMPANIONSHIP

You who dwell in the gardens, the companions
listen for your voice—let me hear it!

Solomon wants to hear her voice. He mentioned this before, in 2:14. He desires her companionship and longs to hear what she has to say and what she feels in her heart.

*Make haste, my beloved, and be like a gazelle
or a young stag on the mountains of spices.*

These final words from the lips of Abishag are an invitation to celebrate their sexual and romantic love. Similar words were spoken in 2:17 and 4:6. In chapter 2 she desired to be alone with him and looked forward to the time when they could be on the mountains of Bether, which means "separation." In chapter 4 he speaks of his time with her as being like the sweetest perfume to his nostrils, an absolute delight to his heart. Now, in these final words, she refers to the "mountains of spices," a clear connection to the words of 4:10,11,14-16; 5:1; and 8:2. Her sexuality was emphasized by these "spices" which would flow from her.

The words "Make haste, my beloved" reveal how important sexual love and romance are to any marriage. We should not be apathetic and indifferent to this need, nor slow to respond to our partner's desires. It's time to "make haste"!

FINAL WORDS ABOUT ROMANTIC LOVE

We have personally learned a great deal from this book, and will continue to do so as we study it in the years ahead. Here are the most important insights that have come to us about romantic love.

1. Sexual pleasure is one of the purposes of marriage.
2. Sexual pleasure within marraige has the approval of God.
3. Premarital sex and extramarital sex are condemned by God.
4. Communication is essential to romantic love.

5. Husbands must praise their wives in order to experience romance in their marriage.
6. Wives must respond enthusiastically to their husbands sexual desires.
7. Commitment is essential for sexual satisfaction and contentment.
8. Inward character is more important than outward beauty.
9. There are no limitations to sexual desires and activities within marriage.
10. Public wedding ceremonies are necessary to confirm the commitments made in marriage.
11. A woman's body is to be admired, praised, and enjoyed by her husband.
12. A man's body is to be admired, praised, and enjoyed by his wife.
13. We should never refuse to have sex with our spouse.
14. There should be no doubt in the minds of other people as to the commitment and love we have toward our spouse.
15. God's love is based on strong commitment and is produced in us by the Holy Spirit.

We have been discouraged at times by couples' neglect of romance. At some point in your marriage this will produce results that you do not expect right now. Do not take your marital partner for granted. Spend time with your spouse developing your intimacy. Get excited about times of sexual love no matter how old you are or how long you have been married.

We think marriage is the greatest! God's love can make it wonderful. We have had our difficulties from time to time during the years of our marriage, but none of these have driven us to the divorce court!

We have tried to follow God's Word in all we do within our marriage and family. It is not always easy; we are so prone to selfishness, wanting our own way. But as we look back over the years, we have wonderful memories and much joy in what God has done because of our commitment to Him and to each other. Our prayer is that you will also see what God can do in your marriage. As you commit your life completely to Him, you will experience His wonderful love!

BIBLIOGRAPHY

Burrowes, George. *A Commentary on the Song of Solomon.* London: The Banner of Truth Trust, 1960.

Carr, G. Lloyd. *The Song of Solomon.* Downers Grove: Inter-Varsity Press, 1984.

Delitzsch, F. *Commentary on the Old Testament,* Vol. 6. Grand Rapids: Wm. B. Eerdmans Publishing Co., 1982.

Dillow, Joseph C. *Solomon on Sex.* Nashville: Thomas Nelson Publishers, 1977.

Glickman, S. Craig. *A Song for Lovers.* Downers Grove: InterVarsity Press, 1978.

Guthrie, D.; Motyer, J.A.; Stibbs, A.M.; and Wiseman, D.J. *The New Bible Commentary: Revised.* Grand Rapids: Wm. B. Eerdmans Publishing Co., 1970.

Harman, Henry M. *Introduction to the Study of the Holy Scriptures.* New York: Hunt & Eaton, 1878.

Hastings, James. *Dictionary of the Bible.* Edinburgh: T. & T. Clark, 1909.

Heydt, Henry J. *The King of Kings in the Song of Songs.* Orangeburg: American Board of Missions to the Jews, 1979.

Ironside, Harry A. *The Song of Solomon.* Neptune: Loizeaux Brothers, Inc., 1933.

Kidwell, R.J., and DeWelt, Don. *Ecclesiastes and Song of Solomon.* Joplin: College Press, 1977.

LaBotz, Paul. *The Romance of the Ages.* Grand Rapids: Kregel Publications, 1965.

Nee, Watchman. *Song of Songs.* Fort Washington: Christian Literature Crusade, 1965.

Pfeiffer, Charles F., and Harrison, Everett F. *The Wycliffe Bible Commentary.* Chicago: Moody Press, 1962.

Tenney, Merrill C. *The Zondervan Pictorial Encyclopedia of the Bible,* Vol 5. Grand Rapids: Zondervan Publishing House, 1975.

Other Good Harvest House Reading

GOOD MARRIAGES TAKE TIME
by *David and Carole Hocking*

Filled with teachings rooted in God's Word, this sensitive book offers help in four areas of married life: communication, sex, friends, and finances. Questions throughout the book for both husbands and wives to answer.

GOD'S BEST FOR MY LIFE
by *Lloyd John Ogilvie*

Not since Oswald Chambers' *My Utmost for His Highest* has there been such an inspirational yet easy-to-read devotional. Dr. Ogilvie provides guidelines for maximizing your prayer and meditation time.

THE DYNAMIC DIFFERENCE
The Holy Spirit in Your Life
by *David Hocking*

Christians often talk about the inner peace and joy we are supposed to experience through Jesus Christ. Too often, however, instead of experiencing the joy of the Lord, Christians are plagued by discouragement and doubt. Why? Bestselling author and Bible teacher David Hocking says the key lies in our understanding of who we are in Christ and what it means to be Spirit-filled. *The Dynamic Difference* will help you discover and experience what it means to have God's power in your life.

AFTER EVERY WEDDING COMES A MARRIAGE
by *Florence Littauer*

Learn how to maintain marital harmony through the trials of marriage. Florence discusses the complexities of marriage and suggests ways to overcome difficulties that can threaten a relationship.

FAMILY PERSONALITIES
The Dynamics and Impact of Family Relationships
by *David Field*

Can you identify your family's "personality"? Every family has one,
says Christian marriage and family therapist David Field, and
yours could be • authoritarian • permissive • chaotic • protective
• sociable • close-knit ... Personality patterns are deeply rooted and
pass from generation to generation, even as new patterns emerge.
Family Personalities helps identify these patterns and provides help
for strengthening the good and changing the not-so-good. Case
studies show how families with differing personalities function,
and the author gives valuable guidance to those who want to raise
their children as God intends—free from past mistakes.

OVERCOMING HURTS AND ANGER
by *Dr. Dwight Carlson*

Dr. Carlson shows us how to confront our feelings and negative
emotions in order to experience liberation and fulfillment. He
presents seven practical steps to help us identify and cope with our
feelings of hurt and anger.

FOREVER MY LOVE
by *Margaret Hardisty*

Margaret Hardisty explains what a woman wants and needs from
her man, and how very much she is willing and eager to give in
return. An inspirational bestseller, there are over 325,000 copies of
Forever My Love in print.

Dear Reader:

We would appreciate hearing from you regarding this Harvest House nonfiction book. It will enable us to continue to give you the best in Christian publishing.

1. What most influenced you to purchase *Romantic Lovers*?
   - ☐ Author
   - ☐ Subject matter
   - ☐ Backcover copy
   - ☐ Recommendations
   - ☐ Cover/Title
   - ☐ _____

2. Where did you purchase this book?
   - ☐ Christian bookstore
   - ☐ General bookstore
   - ☐ Department store
   - ☐ Grocery store
   - ☐ Other

3. Your overall rating of this book:
   - ☐ Excellent   ☐ Very good   ☐ Good   ☐ Fair   ☐ Poor

4. How likely would you be to purchase other books by this author?
   - ☐ Very likely
   - ☐ Somewhat likely
   - ☐ Not very likely
   - ☐ Not at all

5. What types of books most interest you?
   (check all that apply)
   - ☐ Women's Books
   - ☐ Marriage Books
   - ☐ Current Issues
   - ☐ Self Help/Psychology
   - ☐ Bible Studies
   - ☐ Fiction
   - ☐ Biographies
   - ☐ Children's Books
   - ☐ Youth Books
   - ☐ Other _____

6. Please check the box next to your age group.
   - ☐ Under 18
   - ☐ 18-24
   - ☐ 25-34
   - ☐ 35-44
   - ☐ 45-54
   - ☐ 55 and over

Mail to: Editorial Director
Harvest House Publishers
1075 Arrowsmith
Eugene, OR 97402

Name _____

Address _____

City _____   State _____   Zip _____

Thank you for helping us to help you in future publications!